Prison Ramen

Prison Ramen

RECIPES and STORIES from BEHIND BARS

Clifton Collins Jr.
and
Gustavo "Goose" Alvarez

With a Foreword by Samuel L. Jackson

WORKMAN PUBLISHING • NEW YORK

Library of Congress Cataloging-in-Publication Data is available.

ISBN 978-0-7611-8552-9

Design by Lisa Hollander

PHOTO CREDITS:

Cover: Estevan Oriol. **Courtesy of Gustavo "Goose" Alvarez:** p. vi. **Fotolia:** alswart, pp. 8–9, 20–21, 29, 30–31, 34–35, 118–119, 144–145; Avantgarde pp. 5, 7, 14–15, 23, 28, 37, 41, 49, 55, 59, 69, 99, 111 (background), 112–113, 115, 133 (top left), 143, 147; Paco Ayala p. 154; beawolf pp. 6–7, 26–27, 28, 124–125, 152–153; Les Cunliffe p. 45; Zhu Difeng pp. 90–91; fagat pp. 9, 30, 33, 61, 75, 95, 105, 131, 137, 141, 145, 151; Hortiguela pp. xxii, 1; jules p. v; Andrey Kuzmin pp. x–xi, xii–xiii, xx, 3, 17, 31, 44, 45, 47, 57, 71, 87, 101, 107, 113, 122 (top), 125, 128 (top right), 129 (buttons), 130–131, 146–147, 153; Lizard pp. 2, 16–17, 38–39, 42–43, 44, 46–47, 58–59, 70–71, 88–89, 102–103, 120–121, 122 (background), 126–127, 128 (background), 138–139, 148–149; longquattro pp. 92–93; malekas p. xiv; Stanislav pp. 4–5, 132–133, 150–151; Vadim Yerofeyev pp. 11, 25, 53, 67, 73, 77, 85, 97, 110 (top left), 133 (top right), 149; Tamas Zsebok p. xiv. **Getty Images:** Daniel Boczarski p. 58; David Buchan p. 68; Larry Busacca p. 27; Matthew Carr p. 112; Charley Gallay/Getty Images for CineVegas p. 130; Steve Granitz/WireImage p. 40; Chelsea Lauren p. 36; Estevan Oriol/Archive Photos p. 18; Albert L. Ortga p. 14; Rich Polk/Getty Images for Homeboy Industries p. 127; Chris Weeks/Getty Images for 2013 Latinos de Hoy Awards p. 84. **Courtesy of Frank Meeink:** p. 38. **Rex USA:** Everett p. 80.

Workman books are available at special discounts when purchased in bulk for premiums and sales promotions as well as for fund-raising or educational use. Special editions or book excerpts can also be created to specification. For details, contact the Special Sales Director at the address below, or send an email to specialmarkets@workman.com.

Workman Publishing Company, Inc.
225 Varick Street
New York, NY 10014-4381
workman.com

WORKMAN is a registered trademark of Workman Publishing Co., Inc.

Printed in the United States of America

First printing October 2015

10 9 8 7 6 5 4 3 2 1

I DEDICATE THIS BOOK TO MY PARENTS.
FORGIVE ME FOR BEING A THIEF
OF YOUR DREAMS,
BUT THANK YOU FOR SHOWING ME
WHAT UNCONDITIONAL LOVE
REALLY MEANS.
—G.A.

TO MY GRANDPARENTS,
PEDRO GONZALEZ GONZALEZ AND
LEANDRA AGUIRRE GONZALEZ.
WITHOUT THEIR LOVE AND UNDERSTANDING,
WHO KNOWS WHERE I'D BE TODAY.
AND TO JOSH HUTTENBERGER
5/25/1996–11/1/2014.
—C.C.

CDCR
PRISONER
I left my nut in San Diego.

Acknowledgments

FROM GUSTAVO "GOOSE" ALVAREZ:

Clifton Collins Jr., I'm eternally grateful to have you in my life; you are a true friend.

Special thanks to my loving sister, Sandra Luna, for supporting me during my lowest points, giving me hope at those times when I felt hopeless, and, of course, keeping the flame lit for this project in ways too numerous to list.

To Kenia, with faith all things are possible. Love you always.

To Pastor Phil Serrano and Dave Mojaro, behind bars. During the darkest hours of my life, a word of encouragement from you would brighten my day, giving me steady hope.

Thank you to my lovely children for their patience and love while they watched their dad involve himself in a project that probably didn't make a lot of sense to them at the time.

To any youngster on the brink of detention: Heed my lessons. I dedicate this book to you also, with great love and respect.

FROM CLIFTON COLLINS JR.:

To my sister Veronica, for being that moral compass in times when I could not find my way.

To Pat Barrett, for showing me the value of a big bro and mentor at such a young age.

To my boy Goose, who pitched this idea in the visitation yard with the smell of burnt prison dorms still fresh in the air.

Special thanks to my long-trusted friend and lawyer, David Krintzman, for always believing in me and having a solution to seemingly never-ending obstacles. Danielle Josephs, whose presence and hard work would always get us through the day. Tim Cadiente, for his creative support throughout the years and passion for our project that kept us going in times when we thought we couldn't. The Agency Groups' Marc Gerald, for taking a chance on this way out-of-the-box project. Molly Derse, for her kind, caring ways. And, of course, that beast of a house Workman Publishing, with Mary Ellen O'Neill, a passionate talent, collaborator, and godsend; and Selina Meere, with her publicity wisdom. And a giant thanks to all my friends for contributing to this book. I love you guys!

Clifton Collins Jr.

Contents

3
Gen Pop

Page 91

Foreword

Hunger! Quite possibly the first thing we feel entering this thing called life. A breast or a bottle quells it in the beginning, but it always returns, nagging, nagging, nagging, throughout our existence. Some of us have been fortunate enough to beat it back on the regular, others not so much. I've been on both sides of that pronouncement. As a kid, I was well fed by my Southern grandparents, aunts, and neighbors. In the summers, I was on a farm where all I could eat was right at hand. I could pick apples, pears, corn, berries, or anything that grew within my reach. It wasn't until I left home in pursuit of my future that I met real hunger, the hunger that won't let you sleep, study, or think about anything but hunger. Being broke makes you hungrier; it also makes you inventive and creative. Trix with water or Kool-Aid can be tasty. A stolen loaf of bread with mayo, scrumptious! Sardines and crackers, a righteous feast! But nothing prepared me for the inexpensive, filling, soul-refreshing discovery of Ramen and the wonders and complete joy it would bring at my lowest and hungriest times of need. These recipes make me smile and laugh out loud with joy, memory, and awe at their total culinary genius. All born from a bond of pure hunger!

—SAMUEL L. JACKSON

Introduction

One hot day in August, there was a prison riot at the California Institution for Men in Chino. I was halfway through a six-year sentence, the father of young children, and I wanted nothing to do with extending my time in that hellhole. But the race riot that unfolded that night was inescapable.

I was with a group of Southern California Hispanics, outnumbered and trapped in the last surviving dorm. Fires raged all around us. More than one hundred angry men were doing everything possible to break down a secured door. Their only desire was to maim or preferably kill us. We were pretty much doomed—we knew it, they knew it. The only thing I had left in that shithole worth fighting for were the pictures of my kids taped to my locker shelf. So we prepared ourselves for the massacre, lacing up and wrapping towels around our necks to protect our jugulars. There were two Christian brothers in our dorm just praying. It was pretty grim.

And then, as the door began to give way and the rioting inmates were just about to storm in, two older guys ran to our aid. They were OGs—Original Gang members of the Crips—and they stood between us and the bloodthirsty attackers.

They must have argued for two hours, until finally the rioting inmates backed down. The lines of race and gang affiliation are deeper in prison than anywhere else, so the fact that these African American guys defended us—Hispanics—against their own brothers is practically unheard of.

Since fires were still raging, and the door to our dorm was now jammed, we and our "enemies" were both trapped. They were outside in the prison yard, freezing and huddled up. I noticed one of the OG men passing them the little bit of food he had, from his locker. At that moment I felt it only right to try to return a small portion of a big favor. I gathered all the homies and we began to cook all our Ramen and commissary. We made huge spreads, jugs of coffee, and snacks. We shoved all the blankets and mattresses we could fit through the door they had once attempted to break down to kill us. Most of them were just kids, barely in their twenties, living and following the same lies we were.

Shortly after this, I received a visit from my childhood friend Clifton. Growing up in the mean streets of West L.A., who would have thought that many years later we'd still be friends? We came from the same housing projects, but grew up in different worlds. Cliff was never deep in the game like many others, but he was always in the mix. Squabbling, getting shot at, holding his own in street fights like the rest of us. Then he'd bounce the spot and go to an audition. I'd get snatched from the spot and go to juvenile hall. This went on for many years—casting calls for him, county jails for me; movie deals for him, state and federal prisons for me.

Through it all, we maintained our friendship through letters, phone calls, and visits, always holding the dream that one day we'd collaborate on something. I pitched this idea to Cliff when he visited me after the riot and now it's a book in your hands. Take it from someone who knows what he's talking about—you can change your life from wherever you are right now.

—GUSTAVO "GOOSE" ALVAREZ

On August 8, 2009, I was in Iowa finishing up a heavy scene for a film I was doing with Adrian Brody and Forrest Whitaker called *The Experiment*. It's loosely based on Philip Zimbardo's Stanford prison experiment of 1971, in which regular citizens were assigned the roles of guards and prisoners for a psychological study—to disastrous effect.

This particular night was the scene of the big uprising, the convicts against the newly corrupt guards who had become sadistic. Shooting this scene was unusually tense because the director had taken off for a week and we were left to shoot, act, and riot on our own. There were some injuries, but we dealt with them and lived to tell the story.

The following morning I got the news that while I was shooting a riot scene in a movie, my boy Goose was fighting for his very life. I felt sick and wished I could have been there to get his back, as he has always had mine. The odds have never been in his favor, but somehow he has always managed to prevail; I hoped this was one of those times.

Never getting a straight story from news outlets, I did everything I could to get the real story. I took to Twitter and asked hood friends who lived in the area. I heard grisly details about point-blank shootings and convicts getting sliced open with makeshift swords of broken windows, but no Goose.

Just when I feared the worst, I got news that he was all right. We got on the phone and I made plans to go out and see him. He told me of the event that occurred—a meal shared rather than bodies destroyed. I could hear the amazement and pride in his voice. Everything was going to be all right.

—CLIFTON COLLINS JR.

About the Recipes

In prison, having money in your commissary account is the difference between the misery that comes with a flavorless, horribly predictable life, where there is little creativity, and one in which you could travel to places of your youth by imitating the meals your mother made. With a little money, you could show some appreciation for your friends by hosting a spread that lets you all feel like humans rather than numbers for a while. Food items at the commissary are nothing like you'll find in a gourmet shop. Obviously, we didn't have anything that came in a metal can—it would need to be opened with a weapon and then it would become a weapon itself—so you'll see reference to pouches and various prepared items that you may not be able to find in your local store, but you'll find something close enough.

Cooking in prison is much different from cooking in the comforts of home. For one, in prison you don't have the luxury of cooking with proper utensils. Microwaves in prison are weak, so the timing should be adjusted for more modern microwaves. Bags from pork skins or rinds were a useful cooking tool because boiling water never melted the bag. Large buckets lined with plastic trash bags would be used to cook huge spreads.

We'd create sauces by combining ingredients available to us. For instance, strawberry jelly mixed with soy sauce made a pretty good teriyaki sauce. Sometimes we'd melt cheese by putting a jar of cheese in boiling water. We worked with what was available, and created the surprisingly tasty dishes you'll find in this book.

1

Accessory to Ramen

AT THE BEGINNING OF YOUR STRUGGLE, WHEREVER THAT MAY BE, OFTEN ALL YOU HAVE ARE THE BASICS. IN PRISON, THAT MAY BE A SINGLE DOLLAR YOU CAN TRADE FOR A PACK OF RAMEN AND A HANDFUL OF CRACKERS. ELSEWHERE, IT MIGHT BE PEANUT BUTTER AND JELLY, BUT NO BREAD. THIS COLLECTION OF RECIPES LETS THE RAMEN SHINE WITH SIMPLE ADDITIONS.

Nuts to Butts

Being processed at the county jail is just about the most humiliating treatment you can experience. You're stripped of your clothes, packed in lines like sardines, and forced to be as close to each other as possible. The officers yell out, "Nuts to butts!" You can probably figure out what this means. Not only is it humiliating, but the smell of all those bodies mixed with fear, regret, and anger is so bad you can't help but gag.

While you're standing there butt naked, you're told to "spread 'em, bend over, and cough." This is to make sure you aren't bringing any contraband into the county facilities. The procedure usually takes a few seconds but I've seen deputies take their sweet time inspecting any orifice they please. It's all about humiliating the prisoners, breaking them down.

Once the process is over, you're handed a sack with a slice of meat and a slice of cheese. I would trade that stinking sack lunch for butt-naked soup any day.

BUTT-NAKED RAMEN SOUP

INGREDIENTS

1 pack Ramen (any flavor)
About 1 cup boiling water

NOTE: You can serve this with a good handful of chips on the side, but sometimes just enjoying it butt naked is best. The soup, that is.

1. Empty the Ramen into a bowl. Set aside the seasoning packet.
2. Add the water. The Ramen should be submerged.
3. Add more or less water as desired.
4. Add the seasoning. Stir, cover, and let sit for 3 to 5 minutes.

Dear John

Two days after my eighteenth birthday, I was sitting in the L.A. County jail waiting for my transfer to the California State Prison in Corcoran. I was trying to wrap my head around the ten years I had just been sentenced to, when mail call came. And there it was: my own Dear John letter. What did I expect? For my eighteen-year-old girlfriend to wait for me to serve a ten-year sentence?

The tension was particularly high that day because homies were coming in all day reporting on the madness and rage on the streets. It was just after four white LAPD cops where acquitted of beating a black guy named Rodney King just short of death. L.A. went crazy with riots for five days of looting, burning, smashing, and crashing when reports got back about a Hispanic farmworker getting his head bashed in by some black gang members on his way home from work. I knew a race riot was brewing in my new home.

I was trying to distract myself with thoughts of good food. With items from the commissary and a little help from a "stinger," a makeshift prison heating device using metal plates and electrical wires, I cooked up this surprisingly delicious meal. Unfortunately, it tastes all the better when you know you won't be eating any homemade meals for a very long time.

HOT CHILI CORN CHIP PIE

INGREDIENTS

1 pack beef flavor Ramen

1 cup boiling water

1 pouch (9 ounces) or about 1 cup cooked chili beans in hot sauce

1 summer sausage (about 9 ounces), chopped

2 handfuls of corn chips (I find chili-cheese corn chips add optimal flavor.)

NOTE: Any sausage will do, but summer sausage doesn't need refrigeration.

1. Crush the Ramen in the wrapper and empty into a bowl. Set aside the seasoning packet.
2. Add the water, cover, and let sit for 8 minutes.
3. Meanwhile, combine the beans and sausage in a microwavable bowl. Add the seasoning and stir. Cover and microwave for 2 to 3 minutes, until warm.
4. Combine the beans and sausage with the Ramen.
5. Add the corn chips.

WET BEHIND THE EARS

You can tell a first-timer from a seasoned convict by simply observing the way he does his time. A first-timer facing a multiyear sentence will do everything possible to keep communications with the streets alive; a convict facing decades will start cutting all ties. A first-timer will become a phone monster; a convict may get on the phone to make a call on a special holiday or simply send a card. A first-timer will stand and wait by his cell door when he hears the CO passing out mail, and if the CO happens to pass the cell without stopping, it's a sad sight. A convict doesn't trip on mail; he just keeps his mind where his body is, in prison.

As heavy time starts to pass, the first-timer's calls don't get accepted anymore, mail flow starts to slow down, and for some it even stops. Then maybe after a couple of months, sometimes years of this, the famous "Dear John" letter will arrive. Some men can't deal with this and decide to just end it. That's why most convicts know that when facing decades, it's better to cut all ties with the outside world immediately before beginning the long road ahead. Keeping your mind and body in the same place keeps you safe, and sane. It's the only way to do hard time.

INGREDIENTS

1 pack Ramen (any flavor)
Peanut butter
Strawberry jelly

1. Open the wrapper carefully to avoid breaking the Ramen. Save the seasoning packet for another use. Place the square of dry Ramen on a plate.
2. Spread the peanut butter and jelly on the Ramen as you would on a piece of bread.

State Issue

If you find yourself being arrested with no money in your pocket, you're going to be screwed once you get to prison. If you don't have financial support from someone on the outside, you're doubly screwed. Without money, you can't get anything from the commissary, and the commissary is a big part of what makes life worth living. If you were indigent when arrested, you get the "state issue," a collection of crappy supplies—a two-inch toothbrush, toothpaste the size of your pinkie finger that tastes like glue, a body soap that leaves your skin ashy as hell, and a deodorant that burns your pits. If you have long hair, you'll get a state issue comb. Without money, there's no way to get better supplies. Everyone gets a state issue breakfast, sack lunch, and dinner. The menu is usually the same food every day of the week. The food at Corcoran had no salt, no pepper, no spices to give it any flavor. Without money, that's what you'll eat until you gag.

STATE ISSUE SOUP

INGREDIENTS

1 pack chili flavor Ramen
1 cup boiling water
1 slice bologna, chopped
2 slices white bread, cut into quarters
½ cup corn chips

1. Crush the Ramen in the wrapper and empty into a bowl. Add the seasoning.
2. Add the water, stir, cover, and let sit for 8 minutes.
3. Add the bologna, bread, and corn chips. Mix well.

CLOSE CALL

I was in federal prison and looking forward to enjoying this tamale with some friends during a Lakers–Rockets game. I was sitting in the dayroom with the TV, the tamale cooking about twenty feet from me, when a friend bolted around the corner, tossed a cell phone toward me, and whispered, "HIDE IT!" He was clearly being followed, so I stepped quickly and, without a second thought, buried the very small phone inside the tamale. The second the phone was buried, three correctional officers came in and searched the entire area—but skipped the tamale. I was glad to have saved his cell phone, and in gratitude, he gave me all the calls I wanted.

I used that phone all the time. Being able to call my kids and talk to family and friends whenever I wanted was great—for a while. But I started using the phone every day, sometimes staying on it all night. Before I knew it, I was letting the time do me. I still had a few long years to go, and it was turning my life into a living hell. So I had to let it go. It's hard-won wisdom to know the difference between something that feels good in the short term but hurts in the long term.

RAMEN TAMALE

INGREDIENTS

2 packs beef flavor Ramen
1 bag (about 4 ounces) spicy pork skins or rinds
½ cup refried beans
2 bags (1 to 2 ounces each) corn chips
1½ cups boiling water
3 tablespoons squeezable cheese, or more to taste

1. Crush the Ramen in the wrappers. Open the wrappers. Set aside one of the seasoning packets and save the other for another use.
2. Crush the pork skins in the closed bag.
3. Open one end of the bag and add the Ramen, refried beans, corn chips, seasoning, and water. Mix well.
4. Fold the bag in half to secure the tamale. Wrap a towel around the bag to keep the heat in.
5. Let sit for about 30 minutes.
6. Remove the tamale from the bag. Squirt the cheese on top.

SYSTEM OF IDENTIFICATION

When you get to prison you are given an ID with your prison number. When correctional officers want to see what type of inmate they are dealing with, they'll always ask to see your ID. The ID number always begins with a letter. *A* is the oldest, all the way through the alphabet, to *AA* being the newest. You can still see a few old dinosaurs with the *A* letters, pretty much senior citizens by now. They've been in prison over thirty years.

I had a friend, "Richard" from Santa Monica, who was an *A*. He was a *pachuco*. A *pachuco* was a guy who dressed well, went to nightclubs, and lived the high life. Ricky Ricardo from *I Love Lucy* was a *pachuco*. When I met him, he'd been down for thirty-three years. He was charged in the murder of a police officer but still claimed his innocence.

We became close friends because we were both from West L.A., and he enjoyed hearing about the Santa Monica pier and how much the city had changed. I would show him recent pictures and we'd share stories. He told me that after twenty-five years in prison, he'd stopped going to his parole board hearings. He said that no matter what, he would never admit to something he did not do. And all they wanted from him was to admit his guilt. He would say, "God knows the truth; he'll set me free." After our last conversation, Richard was transferred to a federal medical center. Who knows if Richard is still alive. Either way, I hope he's free.

RAMEN BURGER

INGREDIENTS

1 pack beef flavor Ramen

½ cup boiling water

2 hamburger buns or 1 hoagie or hero roll, split open

Mayonnaise

Mustard

Ketchup

Lettuce leaves or shredded lettuce

1 slice onion

2 slices cheese

2 slices tomato

A few hot pickle wheels

1 cooked hamburger patty

NOTE: The hamburger patty would have been smuggled from the kitchen.

1. Open the Ramen wrapper at one end only. Leave the Ramen inside. Set aside the seasoning packet.
2. Hold the open wrapper edge with one hand. With the other, pour the water into the wrapper. Seal with both hands for about a minute.
3. Drain off excess water, leaving only the cooked square of Ramen in the bag.
4. Place the open buns side by side on a plate. Spread the bun halves with mayonnaise, mustard, and ketchup, and top with the lettuce, onion, cheese, tomato, and pickles.
5. Place the hamburger patty in the middle. Place the Ramen square on top.
6. Sprinkle a little of the seasoning on top of the Ramen square. Close up the sandwich.

Instant Karma

BY NEIL BROWN JR.

I was out late in L.A., on my way to see someone my lady would *not* have approved of, if you know what I mean. At 1:00 a.m., I was pulled over by a police car. The officers pulled me out of my car. "Turn around and put your hands behind your back. You have an outstanding warrant." An outstanding warrant? They hadn't even run my damn ID! I wanted to freak out, but deep down I was starting to feel like something else was up. I didn't have any warrants; there was nothing they could possibly find. *Why the hell am I here?*

The officer cuffed me and threw me into the police car. They searched my car, coming up with nothing and clearly getting frustrated. Then another car pulled up. I was bracing myself for the worst. Instead, the officer grabbed my wallet and ran my ID. Then he came over and opened the car door, took the cuffs off, looked me in the eye, and said, "Thank you for your time. Stay out of trouble." That was it. He never told me why I was detained, and the so-called warrant evaporated. They all gave me a look that said, "You need to go *home* now."

In all, I was detained for nearly two hours. Yes, I was innocent of law-breaking, but now it was too late to step out on my lady as I had been planning to do. I believe it was instant karma, that's why I didn't make a fuss. I kept thinking, *I'm sorry baby. I'll never do this again! I love you!*

NEIL BROWN JR. is an actor who has appeared in many movies and TV series, including the action film *Battle: Los Angeles,* the new independent sketch comedy *King Bachelor's Pad,* and the recent release *Straight Outta Compton: The Story of N.W.A.*

RAMEN INSTANT KARMA

INGREDIENTS

1 pack of chili flavor Ramen
1 cup boiling water
2 tablespoons mayonnaise
2 beef sticks (such as Slim Jim), chopped into bite-size pieces
¼ cup chopped chives
Hot sauce

1. Crush the Ramen in the wrapper and empty into a bowl. Set aside the seasoning packet.
2. Add the water, cover, and let sit for about 8 minutes
3. Drain off excess water.
4. Add the seasoning and mix well.
5. Add the mayonnaise, Slim Jims, and chives. Mix well.
6. Add the hot sauce to taste.

The Killer Green Thumb

Doing time through the years, I "visited" some of the worst prison yards in California. But every once in a while, something good would show itself. One of the things I treasured while serving time at the California Men's Colony in San Luis Obispo was sharing an herb garden with some of the homies. Most of the seeds we planted came from our families. Some came from the correctional officers themselves. Man, we grew some of the tastiest vegetables in prison.

The garden belonged to the West L.A. homies. Pretty soon other guys caught on and made their own gardens. We even shared seeds and bragged about our crops to each other. We used these homegrown vegetables to make our meals that much closer to home cooking. It all ended on the day someone took tomato plant leaves to make a toxic tea, poisoning another inmate. It was tough to watch officers pulling out our crops.

SWEET & CRUNCHY SALAD

INGREDIENTS

2 packs chili flavor Ramen
1 cup water
½ can (12-ounce can) Coca-Cola
1 packet Sweet'N Low
Pinch of garlic powder
½ cup pork skins or rinds
2 tablespoons honey
1 tablespoon butter
1 tablespoon strawberry jelly
1 tablespoon soy sauce
1 tablespoon chili garlic sauce
1 cup packaged salad mix (carrots and cabbage with lettuce works well)

1. Crush the Ramen in the wrappers and empty into a large microwavable bowl. Add the seasoning.
2. Add the water, Coke, Sweet'N Low, garlic powder, pork skins, honey, and butter. Mix well. Cover and microwave for 5 minutes, until the Ramen is soft.
3. Combine the jelly, soy sauce, and chili garlic sauce in a separate large microwavable bowl. Cover and microwave for 3 minutes, until bubbling.
4. Add the Ramen mixture and the salad to the sauce. Mix well.

BREAKING BREAD

BY DANNY TREJO

My fondest memories—if you can call them that—of being incarcerated were the weekends. We'd get a bunch of guys together and lay out a spread. Just breaking bread with friends. We'd get whatever we could scrape up—Ramen, chili, popcorn, even hard-boiled eggs. It was like a potluck or picnic, but prison style.

The weekend spreads helped soothe the disappointment of not getting a visit. No matter how tough you look, when it's visiting day and you know you're not getting one, it's hard. You think about all the people who would have visited you if you weren't a three-time loser. Back when I was in juvenile hall, my mom, dad, sister, brother, and everybody would come visit me. When I hit Youth Authority, visits got thinner. In the pen, my mom was the only one who wrote to me.

The weekend spreads helped me think *That's not important*, this *is important.* My friends, my *camaradas,* were important to me. I knew my family wasn't going to visit, but I'd have a family feeling with my homeboys.

DANNY TREJO. Before he became known for playing the anti-hero in dozens of movies and TV series, Danny Trejo was a drug counselor, often helping teenage kids. His first acting role came when he was called to a movie set to help a kid who had an addiction issue. He helped the kid and was cast in the film. Trejo has said, "Everything good that has ever happened to me has been a direct result of helping someone else."

TREJO'S MACHETE RAMEN

INGREDIENTS

2 packs chili flavor Ramen
1½ cups boiling water
About 1 cup chopped cooked pork sausage (9 ounces)
1 small bag (2 ounces) Doritos (any flavor)
Tabasco sauce
2 bags (4 ounces each) corn nuts (any flavor)
1 tablespoon mayonnaise
½ onion, chopped
1 tomato, chopped
3 jalapeño chiles, chopped
2 tablespoons squeezable cheese

1. Crush the Ramen in the wrappers and empty into a bowl. Set aside the seasoning packets.
2. Add the water, cover, and let sit for 8 minutes.
3. Drain off excess water.
4. Add the seasoning, sausage, Doritos, Tabasco to taste, corn nuts, mayonnaise, onion, tomato, and jalapeños. Mix well.
5. Add the cheese and mix again.

Send Me a Mail-Out!

In the current federal prison system, you're not allowed to carry money. All currency is gained by electronic transfers. An inmate's ID card serves as a debit card. An inmate can purchase items at the commissary or send money home by swiping the ID card. It can also be used for buying stuff from prison-sanctioned mail-order catalogs—clothes, shoes, and sundries that are mailed to you in prison. The money in your account is either sent from someone in the free world, or you earn it doing a job in prison. The legitimate jobs pay from ten cents a day to $150 a month. A lot more money is made by gambling or selling drugs to people in prison.

Sometimes an inmate can rack up some serious debt—hundreds or even thousands of dollars—and will have to pay through a "mail-out." This is when the debtor sends the person he owes payment, with help from an outsider, a money order or cashier's check. Some inmates I've known had accounts of more than $100,000. Now there's a cap on how much money an inmate can have on his books because there was a lot of dirty money washing. An inmate's associate could send him a cashier's check or money order from drug sales or some other illegal act and in turn the inmate could send money elsewhere in the form of a clean federal check. The system was used this way for years. It surprised me how long it took the IRS to finally catch on.

ORANGE PORKIES

INGREDIENTS

1 pack Ramen (any flavor)
1 cup boiling water
1 cup cooked white rice
About 3 tablespoons unsweetened orange flavor Kool-Aid
1 bag (about 6 ounces) pork skins or rinds

NOTE: For spicier flavor, try a dash of hot sauce on top of the porkies.

1. Crush the Ramen in the wrapper and empty into a large bowl. Save the seasoning packet for another use.
2. Add the water, cover, and let sit for 8 minutes.
3. Drain off excess water.
4. Add the rice and stir well. Set aside.
5. Pour the Kool-Aid into a large microwavable bowl and add a tablespoon or two of hot water. Stir until it has a syrupy consistency.
6. Toss a handful of pork skins into the syrup and stir. Repeat until all pork skins are coated.
7. Cover and microwave the pork skins for about 5 minutes, until they puff.
8. Serve the pork skins on top of the Ramen and rice.

Lock It Up

When an inmate has a disagreement with another inmate of the same race, often on the basketball or handball court, insults and vicious words get exchanged. Instead of fighting in the yard and risking getting shot, it's common for any of the older homies to yell out "Lock it up!" Once rec yard is over, the two guys, not wanting to attract any attention, will nonchalantly walk into either one's cell, close the door, and fight it out until one guy quits or can't get up. During this dispute, there's always a homie right outside the cell door keeping watch. In most cases, the officers are already aware of the rumble. All they ask is for us to clean up the mess and not use weapons. Sometimes the officer doing his rounds and checking the cells is the one who locks you in and supervises the fight.

These fights between homies allow us to settle our differences without getting shot or causing lockdowns. The officers prefer it to dealing with something bigger and out of control like a riot.

ONION TORTILLA RAMEN SOUP

INGREDIENTS

1 pack chili flavor Ramen
1 cup boiling water
½ onion, chopped
½ cup tortilla chips
1 tablespoon onion powder
1 tablespoon garlic powder
1 jalapeño chile, chopped

1. Crush the Ramen in the wrapper and empty into a microwavable bowl. Add the seasoning.
2. Add the water and stir.
3. Add the onion, tortilla chips, onion powder, garlic powder, and jalapeño. Mix well.
4. Cover and microwave for about 2 minutes, until hot.

REGULATED DUEL

Just about the stupidest and most unnecessary thing you can do in prison is to get into an argument with a correctional officer, and yet it happens all the time. It's especially stupid if the commanding officer is a strict rule follower and a known inmate hater. I knew someone who ended up with an assault charge by spitting on the CO accidentally when they were yelling at each other. Spitting on an officer in or out of prison is considered a form of assault because of the possibility of infecting him with some type of germ. This is obviously bullshit, but according to the rules and regulations of the prison, it's an assault charge and can get years added to your sentence.

First you go to the Hole. Then you have the equivalent of a court hearing with the captain to determine if this "spitting" was an actual assault. You'll be checked by the medical staff to see if you have TB or any other infectious disease. If you're cleared by medical, the captain will usually drop the charge and just keep you in the Hole for thirty to sixty days.

SPAM'EN SOUP

INGREDIENTS

1 pack chili flavor Ramen
1 cup boiling water
½ can (12-ounce can) Spam (any flavor), chopped
½ red onion, chopped
1 jalapeño chile, chopped
1 tablespoon chopped garlic

1. Crush the Ramen in the wrapper and empty into a microwavable bowl. Add the seasoning.
2. Add the water, stir, cover, and let sit for 8 minutes.
3. Add the Spam, onion, jalapeño, and garlic and stir.
4. Cover and microwave for 1 minute, until hot.

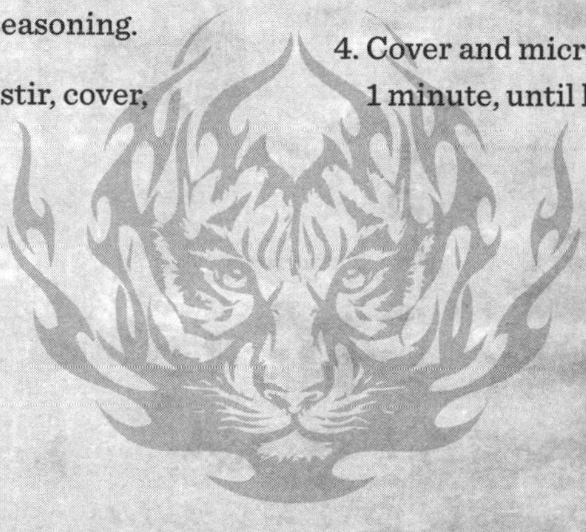

Hard Rock, Hard Time

BY SLASH

It was the really early days of the band. One minute, Duff, our bassist, was driving the band down Melrose Avenue in broad daylight, and the next minute police were pulling us over and taking us in, and I didn't even know why. I ended up in a holding cell, handcuffed to some other guy. Then I was packed into a big black-and-white county bus with a bunch of guys and given no explanation for where we were going. We drove around the entire day, late into the night, and continued until the early morning. We were dropping off all these guys at their city courthouses. We finally got back to L.A. County, and it took all day for me to get processed. By the time I got into my cell—a big community cell—it was nighttime again.

I had on fingernail polish and used my teeth to take all that shit off. I had to. You don't wear nail polish in county jail! I was so miserable, jonesin' really hard, and with all kinds of fools from the weekend's arrests. They kept us in these smelly holding cells until they had enough guys to pack the hot, stinky bus again. I started sweating that nasty, kicking, hungover smell. I couldn't eat, couldn't drink, and had the shivers. The worst feeling ever! This feeling had nothing to do with jail. It's about kicking (withdrawal) and you can't do anything about it. I had no lawyer to call, and I felt like my life could be in danger if I stayed there any longer. L.A. County jail is no joke. Finally, I was called up by a deputy.

Someone—Axl—had put up the bail money to get me out. We had just signed a record deal, but had no record yet and not much money. I was finally told that I had been detained for a jaywalking ticket from high school. For walking across Fairfax and Beverly! Man, that was a long time ago and I had totally forgotten about that.

Apparently *they* don't. To those of you who don't bother with those minor infractions and choose to ignore tickets, beware. There might be a stinky holding cell waiting for you. Word to the wise: Pay your jaywalking tickets.

SLASH is a rock guitarist, songwriter, and film producer whose albums have sold more than 100 million copies. He won a Grammy Award and was inducted into the Rock and Roll Hall of Fame with Guns N' Roses. His autobiography, *SLASH*, was a *New York Times* bestseller.

SLASH'S JAYWALKING RAMEN

INGREDIENTS

1 pack chicken flavor Ramen
1 cup boiling water
3 scallions, chopped
½ cup cooked minced pork
1 tablespoon sriracha sauce, or to taste

NOTE: This recipe is still a favorite snack on the tour bus.

1. Crush the Ramen in the wrapper and empty into a bowl. Add the seasoning.
2. Add the water, stir, cover and let sit for 8 minutes.
3. Mix in the scallions and pork.
4. Add the sriracha to taste.

KILLING FOOD

BY ROGER AVARY

It was my hundredth day in prison. The meal that night in the commissary was shit-on-a-shingle—aka beef tips with gravy—which I couldn't stand to smell, let alone eat. I had saved some rice from my lunch. I never went to chow without my trusty plastic bag. It fit just about a cup's worth of food or condiments so it can be easily smuggled back to the cell. It helped deal with those late-night hunger pangs.

The Jailhouse Hole Burrito is a monster, *my* monster. And let me tell you something, eating this monster was work. To "celebrate" my hundred days, I'd made it so big that I had to attack it like an athlete. Halfway through this particular incarnation, I looked like I was on an episode of *Man v. Food,* and food was winning. I was sweating, and my vision began to tunnel. Between every bite, I was gasping for oxygen like a dying fish. But I made this monster, so I was going to eat it.

I woke up the next morning sick to my stomach. I hadn't eaten that much crap food in a long time, and frankly I was relieved to have survived the ordeal. All I remember from the night before is lying on my bunk in the Ventura County jail, crawling under the sheets and slipping into a food coma. I think if someone had shanked me in the belly that night, I would have exploded Cheetos-flavored Ramen onto them.

I invite you to enjoy this as much as I did, and to recover quickly.

ROGER AVARY is the Academy Award–winning screenwriter of *Pulp Fiction*, *Silent Hill*, and *Beowulf*. He directed the crime thriller *Killing Zoe* and the teen drama *The Rules of Attraction*. Avary supports projectavary.org, dedicated to improving life outcomes for at-risk children with parents in prison.

AVARY'S JAILHOUSE HOLE BURRITO

INGREDIENTS

1 pack Ramen (any flavor)

Hot water

1 large bag (about 8 ounces) jalapeño popcorn (or any bag big enough to hold your ingredients)

½ cup hot sauce

About ½ cup squeezable cheese (jalapeño flavor is popular, but any squeezable cheese is fine)

Handful of cheese crackers

Handful of Takis, Doritos Dinamita, or other spicy rolled chips

1 small bag (about 1 ounce) Cheddar Jalapeño Cheetos, or any spicy flavor

1 large flour tortilla

1. Bust up the Ramen in the bag. There's a jailhouse trick for this, to avoid damaging the bag: Hold the bag of Ramen flat in your palm and with firm but gentle force, throw it flat onto the ground. Repeat this on the other side.
2. Carefully open the bag by one of the top sealed edges, so it forms a pouch.
3. Remove the seasoning packet. Gently and neatly tear off the top of the foil pack and twist it to create a twist tie for the Ramen

bag. Set aside both the open seasoning packet and the twist tie.

4. Pour about a cup of hot water from your sink (which is probably lukewarm) into the Ramen bag. Don't fill it all the way.

5. Twist the bag closed and tie it with the twist tie you created from the seasoning packet.

6. To create a vessel to mix your other ingredients, empty out three-quarters of the popcorn from your large bag. Save that popcorn for later.

7. Take the bag with the remaining popcorn and add the hot sauce, Ramen seasoning, ¼ cup of the cheese (about half), the cheese crackers, and the Takis.

8. Crush up your Cheetos in the bag until they resemble the size of hamburger meat. Add to the mixing bag.

9. Squeeze the rest of your cheese onto a tortilla, slathering it like sauce on a pizza.

10. Drain your Ramen, if necessary, and add to the larger bag. Mix.

11. Now place the fluorescent orange concoction on your prepped tortilla and roll it up, folding the bottom first like a burrito.

DON'T FORGET THE BIRDBATH

You might think that inmates are a bunch of angry, smelly men. And sometimes we are. But I will say this, we do attempt to keep clean—for our own benefit as well as those around us. When we're in a lockdown, cellmates might have to spend weeks, even months, in the cell together. We don't go out or get any air at all and we get only one shower per week. But there is a convict rule that is strictly enforced—by the convicts. Everyone takes a daily birdbath.

While your cellmate stays out of your way on his bed, you fill the sink with water. You can even use the toilet water if you must, but that can be kind of depressing because most of the plumbing is interconnected and you can get some unwanted surprises as a result. Some of the guys will put up a makeshift curtain of bed sheets. Once the sink is filled, use a bowl or cup to pour water on your body. Soap up the major spots, rinse off, and clean up all your mess as a courtesy to your cellmate.

On a very hot summer day, this is done throughout the day. You do what you can to stay cool and clean. There's no telling how long you'll be locked down.

KEEP IT FRESH RAMEN

INGREDIENTS

1 pack chicken flavor Ramen
1 cup of boiling water
2 tablespoons lime juice
½ cup of shredded rotisserie chicken
2 tablespoons salsa
1 tablespoon chopped cilantro
Salt and pepper

1. Crush the Ramen in the wrapper and empty into a bowl.
2. Add the water, cover, and let sit for 8 minutes.
3. Drain the water, add the seasoning, mix well, and set aside.
4. In a separate bowl, add the lime juice, chicken, salsa, and cilantro. Mix well.
5. Add to the bowl of Ramen, mix well, and season with salt and pepper to taste.

SUPERCOP

There's always that one officer who takes his job too seriously. This is the guy who goes that extra inch to make the inmates' time as difficult as it can be. A supercop will search your cell and "accidentally" knock over your TV, or make obnoxious sexual remarks about your girlfriend while you're with her in the visiting room. This is the kind of shit that will get a CO stabbed or killed.

Then there are COs who get along fine with the inmates, who just want to finish their eight hours of work and don't mind what inmates do so long as we're following their program and not causing chaos on their shifts. One officer in particular, let's call him Officer Diaz, was like that. He would want us to "clean the yard," as we'd say. He would give us information on child molesters and snitches, and then turn a blind eye as we rolled 'em up—and out of the prison yard. Some would get badly beaten; some left in body bags. It was a system not many in the free world would understand, but it worked.

Just a few months after my release, some of my homies and I were at a local club when I ran into that very officer. The homies with me were also ex-cons and looked more intimidating than me. He didn't recognize me at first, then his eyes lit up like he saw a ghost. I simply said, "What's up, Diaz?" He was looking pretty nervous. Any other inmate would have had a field day with the opportunity to get his hands on a CO outside of the legal system, but I didn't. I remembered what kind of officer he was. I just kept walking by him, winked my eye, and smiled. He smiled back, nodded his head in a form of respect.

SLOPPY RAMEN JOE

INGREDIENTS

2 packs beef flavor Ramen
1½ cups boiling water
1 can or pouch (7 to 11 ounces) ready-to-eat Sloppy Joe
1 summer sausage (about 9 ounces), chopped, or 1 can (9 ounces) Vienna sausage, drained and chopped
½ medium-size onion, chopped
1 jalapeño chile, chopped
3 or 4 hamburger buns, split open

1. Crush the Ramen in the wrappers and empty into a bowl. Set aside the seasoning packets.
2. Add the water, cover, and let sit for about 8 minutes.
3. Drain off excess water.
4. Combine the Sloppy Joe, sausage, onion, and jalapeño in a large microwavable bowl.
5. Cover and microwave for about 5 minutes, until hot.
6. Add the Ramen and seasoning. Mix well.
7. Place the open buns on plates. Cover with the Sloppy Joe–Ramen mixture.

Blanket Call

BY TARYN MANNING

It was 4:00 a.m. in the Valley. I was on my way home from a party, looking forward to fixing up some Ramen, when I saw the lights flashing behind me. That's when my trip started going south. D.U.I. was quickly assessed. By the time I got booked and sent to County, I had missed blanket call by 5 minutes. I was in a very short dress, freezing, mad, and still kind of drunk. All these other girls were under blankets. All I could see were piles of women with the blankets pulled all the way over their heads. They all looked so comfortable, like they were at a big slumber party. Still, I was freaked out, and I started thinking, *Oh my God, who's under there? Are they going to hurt me?* And to top it off, it was freezing. So I politely called out to the cops, "Excuse me? Excuse me!" Then this voice, one of the guards or one of the women, barked out, "SHUT UP! You missed blanket call, so you are going to freeze. Get used to it!" I can still hear that voice yelling at me while I was shivering, my dreams of Ramen so very far away.

TARYN MANNING is a fashion designer and actor who was critically acclaimed for her roles in the films *Crazy/Beautiful*, *8 Mile*, *Hustle & Flow*, and for her role as Pennsatucky in Netflix's *Orange Is the New Black*.

RAMEN IS THE NEW RAMEN

INGREDIENTS

2 packs Ramen (any flavor)
1 cup boiling water

1. Crush one pack of Ramen in the wrapper. Open both packs and empty the crushed Ramen into a bowl. Save the second square of Ramen for another use. Set aside both seasoning packets.
2. Add the water to the crushed Ramen, cover, and let sit for about 8 minutes.
3. Sprinkle both seasonings on top and stir. The seasoned Ramen, like a seasoned prisoner!

PRISON STETHOSCOPE

BY FRANKIE MEEINK

Once you've finished your Soup in the Hole, save the Styrofoam cup and let it dry. Remove the bottom of the cup. Poke a pencil or pen gently through one side of the cup to make a handle. Using the handle, place the larger opening of the cup to your metal door. Put your ear against the smaller hole at the bottom. Form a seal between your head and the cup, and the cup and the door. You now have a stethoscope that you can use to hear the electronic doors being buzzed throughout the segregation building, which allows you to know if the turnkeys (guards) are coming.

We would always have magazines tied with shoestrings that we could pass up and down the whole cellblock, flinging them from under one door to the other. Hidden inside the magazines would be drugs, a single cig, or just a coded message from one gang member to another. If you missed the other guy's door you could pull it back to try again. You could not let the guards see this—so that's why we had the Styrofoam stethoscopes. We could hear the guards coming two or three doors ahead of our cellblock, so we had time to pull the magazines back in.

FRANKIE MEEINK is the author of *Autobiography of a Recovering Skinhead*, an activist, a board member with the organization Life After Hate, and the founder of Harmony Through Hockey, an organization that works to promote tolerance.

FRANKIE'S SOUP IN THE HOLE

INGREDIENTS

1 cup hot water
1 Cup Noodle (any flavor)
1 beef-and-cheese stick (such as Slim Jim)

1. Because there's no boiling water in the Hole, get hot water from the sink, as hot as you can get it. Pour the water over the Ramen, cover, and let sit for about 5 minutes, until the Ramen is as soft as you like it.
2. Break the beef-and-cheese stick into bite-size pieces. Add to the soup and stir well.

Error Breeds Sense

BY SHIA LABEOUF

I have been incarcerated five times. The first time I was only nine years old. It was in Pacoima, California. I was arrested for stealing a pair of Nike Cortezes from a local shop and held for six hours. The second time I was eleven, in the city of Tujunga, California. I was arrested for stealing a Gameboy Pokémon from Kmart. That time, too, I was in a substation for about six hours. The third time I was twenty, in Van Nuys, California. I tried to stab my neighbor and spent two days in jail. While I was there, I at least understood that being in jail is not the move. It sucks ass. The fourth time I was in Chicago and I wouldn't leave Walgreen's, so I was taken to spend the night in jail. For some reason, I had the best sleep ever. The most recent time was 2014, when I was twenty-eight and in New York City. I went to see the play *Cabaret*. I didn't behave very well during the performance and ended up spending twenty-five hours or so behind bars. While there, I did have a terrific egg sandwich.

When I'm nervous in my creativity, I think of my failures in life and in art. Thinking about my screwups loosens the grip of fear. It's freeing to fuck up and to recover.

SHIA LABEOUF is an actor and director who has been working steadily since age twelve. Two of his most recent films in which he stars include *Fury* and *Man Down*.

EGG RAMEN SALAD SANDWICH

INGREDIENTS

1 pack chicken flavor Ramen
1 cup boiling water
3 hard-boiled eggs, chopped
2 tablespoons mayonnaise
1 hoagie or hero roll, split open
2 slices American cheese

1. Crush the Ramen in the wrapper and empty into a bowl. Set aside the seasoning packet.
2. Add the water, cover, and let sit for about 5 minutes.
3. Drain off excess water. Add the seasoning and mix well.
4. Combine the eggs and mayonnaise in a separate bowl. Mash and mix well with a fork.
5. Add the Ramen. Mix well.
6. Open the roll and place the cheese in it.
7. Fill the roll with the Ramen–egg salad.

The Beat of My Own Drum

I have atrial fibrillation. It's basically an irregular heartbeat, and the risk of stroke is five times higher than when you have a regular heartbeat. It can be really nerve-racking to think about, especially when you're behind bars. Several times I fainted in the middle of an intense handball or basketball game. The homies would freak out! I would wake up in their arms as they were rushing me to the infirmary. After several months of this, I finally got approved to see a cardiologist. He wanted to give my heart an electrical shock—a "reset button" to try to get my heart back on track to a normal rhythm. He said it had a fifty-fifty chance of working. Although I was hopeful, I still felt profoundly troubled. I didn't have any family or friends to be with me and I was slowly discovering that my very new faith was the only thing giving me the strength to get by. So I took a moment to say a quick prayer.

While they were prepping me for the procedure, one of the nurses and a younger officer guarding me started to talk dirty to each other.

Just the most outrageous stuff—anal sex, oral sex, and every other kind of sex you could think of. I lay there thinking, *I can't believe my life is in these hands!* Then the door opened and a much older female officer walked in to relieve the young cop. It was like your mom walked into the room where you and your friends were discussing porn. She had a Bible in hand and was flipping through the pages as she sat in a chair just beside the doctors and nurses prepping me.

I went under the anesthesia. It felt like it was only moments later when I was suddenly awakened by a burning sensation to my chest. I could see the doctor looking at my heart monitor, shaking his head. "It doesn't look like it worked." I yelled out, "Try it again!" and told the old female officer holding the Bible, "Pray for me!" I remember her jumping out of her seat, saying, "Okay, honey." She rubbed my arm and I fell back asleep to the sound of her prayers.

Again, I was awakened by a burning shock to my chest. This time I saw everyone in the room smiling and cheering as they looked at the monitor.

FIBRILLATION SALAD

INGREDIENTS

1 head iceberg lettuce, washed, dried, and chopped or shredded

1 tomato, chopped

½ red onion, chopped

½ cup shredded Jack cheese

4 slices ham, cut into bite-size pieces

4 yellow chiles in vinegar (*aji Amarillo*), drained and chopped

1 pack chili flavor Ramen

Salad dressing (any flavor you like)

1. Combine the lettuce, tomato, onion, cheese, ham, and chiles in a large bowl.
2. Crush the Ramen in the wrapper. Pour the seasoning on top of the crushed Ramen in the wrapper. Shake to coat the Ramen.
3. Pour the spiced Ramen over the salad.
4. Add salad dressing to taste and gently toss.

2

Solitary Dining

SOLITARY DINING IS FULL OF RECIPES CREATED MOSTLY IN THE SECURITY HOUSING UNITS. THESE MEALS ARE USUALLY FOR ONE, BUT THEY'RE EASILY STRETCHED TO FEED TWO. MANY OF THE INGREDIENTS USED TO PREPARE THESE DISHES WOULD HAVE BEEN SMUGGLED IN BY CORRECTIONAL OFFICERS OR BROUGHT IN THROUGH APPROVED VENDORS; OTHERS WOULD HAVE BEEN PURCHASED WEEKLY THROUGH COMMISSARY. EVERYTHING IS BROUGHT TO YOUR CELL, JUST LIKE ORDERING A PIZZA. EXCEPT NOT AT ALL.

Everyday Hustle

In the federal prisons, there aren't a lot of jobs for inmates, and what jobs there are don't pay very much. So people got creative. Some would steal food from the kitchen and sell it for a quick come-up. It was amazing how many food items were smuggled out of kitchen storage—vegetables, fruit, bags of sugar, even raw eggs. Some guys got busted, but others were masterful in their techniques. I've seen several different designs for smuggling underwear with pockets sewn into the crotch area and waist belts made from T-shirts.

I knew a guy who would smuggle raw eggs and shredded Jack cheese every Saturday morning. He was a heavyset guy—at least 250 pounds and just a little over five feet tall. His trick was not only wearing his specially designed underwear; he would also rub a dirty towel from the kitchen's mop room all over his clothes so that his odor was repellent. Most officers didn't like to search him for just that reason. This guy made a lot of money smuggling food from the kitchen. Other guys weren't so fortunate. A couple of raw eggs got them a couple of months in the Hole.

RAMEN BEEF & BROCCOLI

INGREDIENTS

2 packs chili flavor Ramen
1½ cups boiling water
½ cup or ¼ pound cooked beef tips (4 ounces)
½ cup steamed broccoli florets (4 ounces)
½ onion, chopped
1 carrot, chopped
6 tablespoons soy sauce

1. Crush the Ramen in the wrapper and empty into a bowl. Set aside the seasoning packet.
2. Add the water, cover, and let sit for 8 minutes.
3. Drain off excess water.
4. Mix the beef tips, broccoli, onion, and carrot in a large microwavable bowl. Add the soy sauce and stir. Cover and microwave for about 5 minutes, until hot.
5. Add the Ramen and half of the seasoning. Mix well.

Along for the Ride

I've met many guys who will be in prison for the rest of their lives. Some of these guys committed violent acts, even taking a life, while others were just along for the ride. One of the latter was a good friend of mine—Robert, aka Big Rob. He was fresh out of high school when he made the mistake of going cruising with his high school friends. Unfortunately, those friends were gang members. They were out for a drive on a summer night when another car from a rival gang pulled up beside them. Gang slurs were exchanged and gunshots rang out. Robert was hiding in the back seat, in a fetal position, scared shitless. Their car sped off but they didn't get more than a few blocks before they were cut off and cornered by the local police. A passenger in the other car had been killed by retaliatory gunfire. Even with no prior convictions of any sort, Robert was charged with accessory to first degree murder and was sentenced to twenty-five to life when he was eighteen years of age.

I met him in 2007 when he was in his early thirties. He wasn't in a prison gang or even associated with one. He'd never had a problem since he was arrested. While in prison he took every class he could, becoming accomplished at many trades and earning degrees. He never used drugs or alcohol. He was a good, square guy. It didn't make sense that he had to serve as much time as the trigger man. Robert and his family didn't have the money to hire a good attorney. He was one of the many poorly represented guys who were railroaded by the "dump truck"—what we call the plea offers from the public defender. Robert paid more than he should have for being a dumb kid.

LONG SENTENCE SOUP

INGREDIENTS

2 packs chili flavor Ramen

1½ cups boiling water

½ cup chopped carrots

½ cup chopped celery

½ cup corn kernels

1 tomato, chopped

1 jalapeño chile, chopped

½ onion, chopped

1 tablespoon garlic powder

½ cup tomato puree (3 tablespoons tomato paste thinned with enough water to make ½ cup also works well)

1. Crush the Ramen in the wrapper and empty into a microwavable bowl.
2. Add the water, carrots, celery, corn, tomato, jalapeño, onion, garlic powder, and tomato puree. Mix well.
3. Cover and microwave for about 5 minutes.
4. Stir, then re-cover and microwave for 5 minutes more, until the Ramen is soft and the soup is hot.

Prison Ink

People get tattoos for different reasons. Some are indulging boredom, others are asserting some control over their own bodies, and many are pledging allegiance to a gang. But for Southern Hispanics, it's a bit more than any of that. We favor Aztec culture tattoos because they represent the life of an Aztec warrior. The warriors fought battles to defend their land, worship the way they chose, and to retrieve prisoners from warring tribes. When an inmate is deemed trustworthy enough to defend his tribe by executing a hit, he knows he risks spending the rest of his life in the SHU. In recognition of the risk and—hopefully—the success, certain tattoos are specific to certain accomplishments. Inmates believe these tattoos represent strength, aggressiveness, and competitiveness.

I got my whole back piece done over two weeks, lying on my stomach for two to three hours at a time. The session took place in a container—like a trailer—used to store weights. There would be two guys standing outside as lookouts while the tattoo artist worked. Halfway through, the tattoo artist and I got into a heated argument that resulted in a vicious fight! He took out his aggression by practically butchering me with his homemade tattoo gun. I made it through and recovered with help from the homies. It's a wonder the infections didn't put me down for good.

CHICKEN HONEY RAMEN

INGREDIENTS

1 pack chicken flavor Ramen
1 cup boiling water
1 summer sausage (about 9 ounces), chopped
2 tablespoons honey

1. Crush the Ramen in the wrapper and empty into a bowl. Set aside the seasoning packet.
2. Add the water, cover, and let sit for 8 minutes.
3. Drain off excess water.
4. Microwave the sausage in a separate bowl until hot.
5. Add the sausage and seasoning to the Ramen and stir.
6. Drizzle the honey on top.

FINAL TIMEOUT

When you get arrested in Los Angeles, your first stop is the city's substation jail—a police station holding cell. If you can't make bail, you're sent to the L.A. County jail. There, the smell attacks you the minute you walk inside. If you don't notice it immediately, it's probably because all you can smell is the stinky ass of the guy in front of you.

If you're not a first-time convict, you'll probably be sent to state prison, where you're surrounded by killers, lifers, and prison gang members. If you get in trouble in prison you go to Administrative Segregation, aka the Hole, either for your own safety or for others'. If you screw up in the Hole—maybe fighting with your cellmate or assaulting an officer—you go to the Security Housing Unit (SHU). This is a single-man cell, and you're handcuffed and escorted by officers wherever you go—even to take a shower. If you need to shave, the officer will hand you a dull disposable razor once you're inside the shower cell. Then the officer will check the razor for its blade upon its return. You are escorted outside to the yard for one hour a day, staying inside what appears to be a large dog kennel. Usually, there are ten kennels in an area about as big as a basketball court, surrounded by fifteen-foot-high walls. Only thing you can see is the sky. If you get into trouble while in SHU, then you end up in the last stop.

Deep Administration Segregation (Deep AD-SEG) is known as your final time-out. It's underground or far away from other cells. You are all alone, with no cellmate or anyone close enough to talk to through the vents. No TV, radio, or any appliance. Just you, four walls, a toilet, and your cement bed. The only light is controlled by officers you can't see or talk to. It's not unusual to be stuck there for a full year. In my experience, most guys who end up in solitary confinement suffer from some type of antisocial disorder.

RAMEN CHOWDER

INGREDIENTS

2 packs shrimp flavor Ramen
1½ cups boiling water
¾ cup prepared clam chowder
½ cup chopped baby carrots
½ cup chopped onion
1 tablespoon garlic powder

1. Crush the Ramen in the wrapper and empty into a bowl. Add the seasoning.
2. Add the water, stir, cover, and let sit for 8 minutes. Do not drain.
3. Mix the clam chowder, carrots, onion, and garlic powder in a microwavable bowl.
4. Cover and microwave for about 5 minutes, until hot.
5. Add to the Ramen. Mix well.

PIMP TO WIMP

In the late 1990s, an inmate was entitled to thirty pounds of groceries every three months from an approved vendor—always one of the local grocers. On visiting day, an inmate's family members would go to the approved grocer, pick up the groceries, and bring them to the inmate. It was the highlight of the month.

Back then, there was a guy who claimed to be a major pimp on the streets, boasting and bragging about all the women he had out there taking care of him. How he was such a player that sometimes he had two women visiting him at the same time, always showing off nude photos of different women. This bragging sometimes went on for hours. One time on our way to package pickup, he kept bragging about his girls and saying things like, "I wonder which of my girls is sending me a package this time" and "Pimping ain't easy but it sure is fun!" This was getting on everyone's nerves. Even the officer had had enough and told him to pipe down with all that bullshit. When this "pimp" was finally called to step up and receive his package, to his and everybody's surprise, his "girl" sent him thirty pounds of canned dog food! The look on this guy's face went from pimp to wimp! His homies couldn't stop clowning him, and even the officers had a good laugh and some shit to say. But turns out the pimp didn't come up empty-handed. The officer passing out the packages offered him twenty bucks for the box of dog food, saying he had two "bitches" at home that would love this care package.

RAMEN, RED POTATO & TUNA TOSS

INGREDIENTS

1 pack chili flavor Ramen

1 cup boiling water

1 can (5 to 6 ounces) tuna, drained

¼ pound small red potatoes, cooked and quartered

½ green bell pepper, seeded and chopped

1½ teaspoons dried dill

¼ cup olive oil

1. Crush the Ramen in the wrapper and empty into a bowl. Set aside the seasoning packet.
2. Add the water, cover, and let sit for 8 minutes.
3. Drain off excess water.
4. Mix the tuna, potatoes, green pepper, dill, olive oil, and seasoning in a large bowl.
5. Add the Ramen. Mix well.

Saltpeter

The L.A. County jail has its urban legends, but one I can say might have been true was about the punch that was served with lunch and dinner. There was always plenty on every table, as it was served in big pitchers, and I always had a few cups with dinner. Three months into my first time in L.A. County, I was finally told by an older homeboy, "Stop drinking the punch; it's not good for you, little homie." He said it was made with a substance called saltpeter, which contained potassium nitrate. Clueless of what he was telling me, I said, "Saltpeter? Potassium nitrate? What the hell is all that?"

He laughed and said, "Okay, let me ask you this. When's the last time you beat your meat?" I asked him what the hell that had to do with saltpeter or potassium nitrate? He said saltpeter is put in the punch in order to suppress our sexual urges. It makes us less violent and keeps us calm. I really couldn't believe what he was telling me, and I just brushed him off. But back in my cell I started to wonder why I hadn't beat my meat in just over three months. Then it started to mess with my head—both heads. I wasn't able to get the usual morning erection as before, and didn't even have the urge to stroke it. That did it.

From then on, I refused to drink that punch. After a few days, as I started to forget about the whole saltpeter thing, I was awakened by the stiffest boner I ever had in my life! Man, it was at attention and saluting proudly. What else could I do but . . . relieve my stress.

SOLDIER'S SALUTE RAMEN

INGREDIENTS

1 pack shrimp flavor Ramen
1 cup boiling water
¼ cup chopped red onion
2 jalapeño chiles, chopped
1 tomato, chopped
Pinch of dried oregano
2 cans (3 ounces each) baby clams, drained
½ avocado, sliced

1. Crush the Ramen in the wrapper and empty into a bowl. Set aside the seasoning packet.
2. Add the water, cover, and let sit for 8 minutes.
3. Drain off excess water.
4. Mix the onion, jalapeños, tomato, and oregano in a separate bowl.
5. Add the Ramen, seasoning, and baby clams. Mix well.
6. Top with the avocado slices.

No Stars Behind Bars

BY DAVID ANTHONY FAUSTINO

Being a celebrity from a hit TV show had its advantages. Dinner at the finest restaurants without a reservation. The front of the line of the hardest clubs to get into. Getting attention from girls I should never get attention from. Also, rarely getting harassed by cops. I'd fly down the 101 like a spoiled little brat, and when I'd get pulled over, they'd say, "Hey. It's Bud Bundy! How's your sister, bro?" No tickets for me in L.A. or anywhere nearby.

Once, my (now ex) wife and I went to visit her family from Daytona Beach, Florida. We went out with some friends one night and I got extremely drunk. I started to argue with my wife in public. It got so bad that three cops swooped down on us. I tried pulling the old "I'm Bud Bundy" shit, but I was such a sloppy, rude drunk, the cops said, "We don't care. You're going to jail." I spent about six hours in a single-man cell. Unbelievably, when they came to get me, I start talking shit again. I called the woman who was booking me all kinds of names. Finally, another officer yelled out, "Yo, dog, I swear to God, shut up or you're back in that cell for a long time!" I shut my mouth and didn't say another word.

After this incident, I cut way back on alcohol. I realized that when I drink too much, I'm nothing more than that loud asshole at the party that no one likes. Who wants to be that guy?

DAVID ANTHONY FAUSTINO is an American rapper who has appeared in dozens of films and television series, and is primarily known for his role as Bud Bundy on the FOX sitcom *Married . . . with Children* from 1987 to 1997, and for voicing Mako in *The Legend of Korra*.

WET RAMEN BURRITO

INGREDIENTS

2 flour tortillas

1 bag (8 ounces) of Cheez-Its, or any other empty plastic chip bag to form the burrito

1 pack chili flavor Ramen

½ cup of Cheez-Its or any cheese cracker

½ cup refried beans

1 summer sausage (about 9 ounces), chopped, or 1 can (9 ounces) Vienna sausage, drained and chopped

1 small bag (about ¼ cup) Cheetos, crushed in bag

1 hot pickle, chopped

1½ cups boiling water

3 tablespoons squeezable cheese, or more to taste

1. Place one flour tortilla, open, inside the bottom of the plastic chip bag.
2. Crush the Ramen in the wrapper. Pour it into the bag on top of the open tortilla.
3. Add the seasoning, Cheez-Its, refried beans, sausage, Cheetos, and hot pickle.
4. Cover the mixture with the other flour tortilla. Wrap the top tortilla together with the bottom tortilla, nice and tight. The bag helps to hold the form of the burrito.
5. Add the water. Carefully fold the bag tightly and let sit for about 8 minutes.
6. When ready, slide the burrito out of the bag and onto a plate, and top it with the squeezable cheese.

The Art of Carrying a Weapon

In the federal prison system, carrying a weapon undetected is an art. There are metal detectors in every officer's hand, and everyone is swiped before entering any building. So inmates came up with a much deadlier weapon, one that's a lot easier to hide from the common metal detector: the razor blade. Masterfully cracking open the plastic housing of a disposable shaving razor with a set of nail clippers, you very carefully remove the delicate blade from the plastic shaver. If used properly, you can slice a man's jugular vein in one quick swipe. Easy to carry, easy to hide. It can be carried in the mouth, sticking to the side of your tongue or against your cheek. The COs never seem to swipe a face with their metal detectors.

RAMEN SPAGHETTI

INGREDIENTS

2 packs beef flavor Ramen
1½ cups boiling water
1 jar or pouch (10 ounces) meatballs in tomato sauce
1 onion, chopped
Pinch of garlic powder

1. Crush the Ramen in the wrappers and empty into a bowl. Set aside one of the seasoning packets; save the other for another use.
2. Add the water, cover, and let sit for about 8 minutes.
3. Drain off excess water.
4. Meanwhile, mix the meatballs, onion, seasoning, and garlic powder in a microwavable bowl.
5. Cover and microwave for 3 to 5 minutes, until hot.
6. Pour the mixture over the Ramen.

Escaping, Forever

For years, outside my cell window stood a huge fence, twenty feet high, covered with razor-tipped barbed wire. I have no doubt that almost every prisoner thought of hitting that fence at least once. Some guys would do more than think about it. For many of us, doing time became worse than the idea of being dead. Those were the ones that would make a run for the fence, hoping to be shot and killed. This was known as "suicide by escape."

I saw it in action in a way that just broke my heart. A good friend of mine was waiting for his family on visitation day. It was the best part of his week and they were very reliable. He'd always leave his time with them with a smile on his face and plenty of goodwill for everyone he ran into. One day, they just didn't show up. He sat there, hour after hour, wondering what the holdup was. They didn't show up all day and didn't answer the phone when he called.

Two days later a guard came to escort him to the chapel where the chaplain gave him the bad news. His family had crashed on the highway on their way up to visit him. His wife, kids, and mother-in-law all died in the accident. There were no survivors. With many years to go in his sentence, he literally had nothing to live for.

Rumors quickly spread that he actually made it over the first fence. But by the second fence, two shots from a Mini-14 rifle gave him his freedom . . . to be with his family.

CALDO DE POLLO (CHICKEN SOUP)

INGREDIENTS

1 pack chicken flavor Ramen
1 cup boiling water
½ cup chopped baby carrots
¼ cup chopped onion
Pinch of garlic powder
½ cup shredded or chopped cooked chicken breast
1 jalapeño chile, chopped

1. Crush the Ramen in the wrapper and empty into a bowl. Add the seasoning.
2. Add the water, stir, cover, and let sit for 8 minutes.
3. Add the carrots, onion, garlic powder, chicken, and jalapeño. Mix well.
4. Cover and let sit until the vegetables are warm.

THE APPRENTICE

BY ALMA BLAKE, FORMER CORRECTIONAL OFFICER

As a former CO, I was a curiosity to the women I was incarcerated with. The first person to befriend me was Colombiana, and she resembled my mother. With her heavy accent she told me, "You see all these women? They all have a trade. They all know how to do or make something to help them get by. We all work at something. What can you do?" I didn't have a response, so she peppered me with questions: " Can you cook prison style? Can you draw? Can you color, gamble, thread eyebrows, sew?" My silence said it all. I didn't know how to do any of those things. She offered me a plate of her delicious food and told me, "Don't worry, Mami, we will find you something to do." I felt ashamed that even though I had worked for over eight years in a prison, I was the most ignorant inmate. Then Colombiana asked, "Can you read and write?" Almost laughing, I said "Yes!" She gave me a piece of paper and told me to write out a recipe she'd dictate. When she saw my handwriting she smiled at me and said, "I think I just found you a job." Colombiana was a fine artist and made greeting cards for anyone in need of a birthday or holiday card, but she had terrible handwriting. I became her apprentice and filled in the greetings on the cards. I would not have made it through my time in prison without her help. We developed a friendship that lasts to this day.

ALMA BLAKE worked as a correctional officer. She served time for an infraction committed while a CO. She now works in a civilian capacity in her hometown of El Paso, TX. She teaches her sons to respect and understand the reasons for the law, with the hope that they may pursue a career in it one day.

RAMEN FOR A NEWCOMER

INGREDIENTS

2 packs chicken picante flavor Ramen
3 cups boiling water
½ teaspoon crushed red pepper
¼ teaspoon garlic powder
½ teaspoon soy sauce
Tortilla chips

1. Place the Ramen into a bowl without breaking it. Add the seasoning.
2. Add the boiling water, crushed red pepper, garlic powder, and soy sauce.
3. Mix well, and let it sit for 8 minutes.
4. When ready, top it with a handful of tortilla chips.

Brother Against Brother

There was a time back in the day when convicts, all dressed in blue, wouldn't fight one another. Instead we'd stand united, fighting against the cops who would be dressed in green. Those days are long gone. We don't have the unity we once had.

A riot can occur at the most unexpected times. It seems to me that racial fighting was the main motivation in most of the riots I saw . . . and participated in. Black against white, brown against black, or brown against white. Sometimes, there was even fighting within the races, but it was still about race. For example, you'd have Mexican immigrants fighting in big riots against the Mexican American homeboys. This discourages me because I feel as if the guys I'm fighting against could be my uncles or my brothers.

These stupid riots between us always stem from some type of drug debt or power trip. I've been in many riots, but riots against my own race have been the most tragic. Lots of stabbing and fighting to the death. Vicious soldiers out to destroy one another, fighting the wrong enemy.

RAMEN BEEF BOWL

INGREDIENTS

1 pack picante beef flavor Ramen

1 cup boiling water

1 summer sausage (about 9 ounces), chopped, or 1 can (9 ounces) Vienna sausage, drained and chopped

1 can (about 12 ounces) ready-to-eat roast beef

1 bag (about 4 ounces) pork skins or rinds

½ onion, chopped

3 jalapeño chiles, chopped

¾ cup soy sauce

¾ cup grape jelly

NOTE: This was often sold in the commissary as "roast beef dinner with gravy." If that's what you find, drain off the gravy.

1. Crush the Ramen in the wrapper and empty into a bowl. Set aside the seasoning packet.
2. Add the water, cover, and let sit for 8 minutes.
3. Drain off excess water.
4. Meanwhile, combine the sausage, roast beef, pork skins, onion, jalapeños, seasoning, soy sauce, and jelly in a microwavable bowl. Mix well.
5. Cover and microwave for about 10 minutes, until hot.
6. Add the Ramen. Mix well.

PRANKING TO PASS THE TIME

BY RUSTY COONES

In 1999 I was rounded up in a federal conspiracy case. An attorney was once quoted as saying, "A grand jury could indict a ham sandwich under federal conspiracy laws." I saw the evidence of that. Eventually, I was sentenced to eight years.

We had our own table where only "our guys" sat. On Sundays they brought out the toasters, but there was always a line waiting to toast bread. So we had a guy who would wait in line for us and toast the bread. We named him the Toastmaster General.

We were always looking for something to break the monotony of doing time. I liked pranking people. I got together with a couple of guys one time and we posted notices on the bulletin boards all over the prison saying it was mattress exchange day. Everyone was required to take his mattress up to the laundry room during yard time before lunch. About a hundred guys lined up at the guard shack, trying to get through the metal detector with their mattresses, until the guards figured out it was a hoax.

RUSTY COONES is the lead guitar player for Attika7, a custom bike builder for Illusion Motorcycles, and a costar on *Sons of Anarchy*.

BAKED CHICKEN RAMEN

INGREDIENTS

1 pack chicken flavor Ramen
½ cup water
½ cup chopped baked chicken breast

1. Crush the Ramen in the wrapper and empty into a bowl. Add the seasoning.
2. Add the water, stir, cover, and microwave for 3 to 5 minutes, until the Ramen is soft.
3. Add the chicken, stir, re-cover, and microwave for 1 minute more.

PRISON BOOTS

Inmates are separated for a variety of reasons, including what is easy to see (race) and what is much more complex (gang affiliation). There's a little prison legend about how two Hispanic groups broke apart. A long time ago, it is said that all California Hispanics were united as one in the California Department of Corrections. Northern and Southern California Hispanics stuck together and were powerful in prison and on the streets. Supposedly, one day in the late 1960s all that changed. A Southern Hispanic gang member accused a Northern gang member of stealing his boots. After weeks of mounting tension, a most vicious riot occurred between the Northern and Southern Hispanics. I'm sure there was more to it than those stinking boots, but my experience is that we Hispanics are a prideful lot, and we don't back down from a disagreement, no matter how ridiculous it is.

To this day, these two sides are worst enemies, both in prison and now on the streets. The only thing other than race they have in common is their stinking, ugly prison boots.

DIRTY RAMEN

INGREDIENTS

1 pack chili flavor Ramen

1 cup boiling water

1 package (5.7 to 8 ounces) microwavable dirty rice

1 summer sausage (about 9 ounces), chopped, or 1 can (9 ounces) Vienna sausage, drained and chopped

½ cup chopped green beans

½ cup chopped carrots

½ cup chopped onion

NOTE: "Dirty rice" is white rice cooked with seasonings. If you can't find it, any flavored microwavable rice will do.

1. Crush the Ramen in the wrapper and empty into a bowl. Set aside the seasoning packet.
2. Add the water, cover, and let sit for 8 minutes.
3. Drain off excess water.
4. Meanwhile, microwave the rice as directed on the package.
5. Add the rice to the Ramen.
6. Mix the sausage, green beans, carrots, and onion in a microwavable bowl. Cover and microwave for 5 minutes, until hot.
7. Add the sausage mixture to the Ramen and rice. Mix well.

No Warning Shots

When I first started doing time in the early 1990s, every gun tower had a sign with the same promise: ONE WARNING SHOT. This meant that if you did not get down when the alarm rang, or as soon as the first warning shot let out, the next shot would have your name on it. Many a time, I'd be eating indoors in the chow hall when a fight would start outside on the yard. The alarm would go off, signifying *get down*. A second later, you'd hear the first warning shot—a Mini-14 rifle aimed out the window of the gun tower toward the sky. The sound was so loud it left your ear drums ringing. It was a real attention-getter.

Gang hits in the late '90s were getting crazier by the day—most of the attacks would continue even after the first shot rang out. Performing a hit this way, with total disregard for the warning shots, is called a "torpedo hit." These acts were usually done by youngsters trying to make a name for themselves. Some were successful in the hit, while others might get shot and end up in worse condition than the guy they were sent out to hit.

During my time at Corcoran, in order to control the boldness of the inmates, staff made it clear that there would be no more warning shots. So then the writing under every gun tower read: WARNING. NO WARNING SHOTS! You better believe they take this shit seriously. There's an officer straight out of the military, specialized as a sniper, just waiting to show off his marksmanship.

RAMEN TORTA

INGREDIENTS

1 pack chili flavor Ramen

1 cup boiling water

1 large hoagie or hero roll
(big enough for two people),
split open

¼ cup mayonnaise

¼ cup mustard

¼ pound sliced turkey

¼ pound sliced ham

¼ pound sliced chicken breast

1 tomato, sliced

1 onion, sliced

About 6 lettuce leaves or a handful of shredded lettuce

¼ pound sliced pepper Jack cheese

1. Crush the Ramen in the wrapper and empty into a bowl. Set aside the seasoning packet.
2. Add the water, cover, and let sit for about 8 minutes.
3. Drain off excess water.
4. Open the roll, leaving the sides attached. Spread the mayonnaise and mustard on the inside of the roll.
5. Spread half of the Ramen on the roll. Sprinkle half the seasoning over the Ramen.
6. Lay the turkey, ham, chicken, tomato, onion, and lettuce on top of the Ramen.
7. Add the rest of the Ramen and sprinkle with the remainder of the seasoning.
8. Top with the cheese. Close gently and hold it down while cutting it in half.

Black and Brown Get Down!

It was a cool afternoon, and I was waiting for my turn to play handball with the homies. We all noticed the scuffle on the other side of the prison yard. Once we saw who was fighting—black and brown—it was like a domino effect. One after another, every black and Hispanic inmate in the vicinity ran toward the square dance. Midway, we were cut off by a few brothers running in from the basketball court. They were squaring up to fight, and it looked like we were outnumbered and outsized. But before they could swing, the two homies I was with pulled out shanks. The square dancing continued and the brothers didn't back down from a knife fight. Finally, there were tear gas shots, rubber bullets, and warning shots to the sky. The goon squad—special task force officers—ran in with zip ties and cuffs, and the riot was contained.

I was lying facedown in the main yard with my hands cuffed, waiting to be placed in AD-SEG (Administration Segregation), where everyone in the riot was headed. All around me I heard moans of agony and pain, but I had managed to avoid being cut or wounded badly. All I could think of at the time was eating a warm bowl of this Spicy Ramen Rice Casserole, a recipe I had just gotten right. Go figure. The stuff we think of in the most unusual circumstances.

SPICY RAMEN RICE CASSEROLE

INGREDIENTS

2 packs chili flavor Ramen
1 cup boiling water
1 package (7.5 to 8.5 ounces) cheesy rice
1 pouch (5 ounces) seasoned beef crumbles or ¾ cup seasoned crumbled cooked ground beef
2 to 3 tablespoons picante sauce, or to taste
1 jalapeño chile, chopped

NOTES:

- Uncle Ben's and Old El Paso both make a cheesy rice.
- Libby's beef crumbles were for sale at the commissary.

1. Crush the Ramen in the wrapper and empty into a bowl. Set aside the seasoning packets.
2. Add the water, cover, and let sit for 8 minutes.
3. Drain off excess water.
4. Meanwhile, prepare the rice as directed on the package.
5. Combine the seasoning, beef, picante sauce (to taste), and jalapeño in a separate bowl. Mix well.
6. Cover and microwave for 5 to 10 minutes, until hot.
7. Mix the beef and Ramen into the rice.

Eyewitness to Mayhem

It was six-thirty on a cool Saturday morning in the California State Prison, Corcoran. My road dog Spider and I were out for our usual morning walk around the yard. Coffee in hand, beanies down past our eyebrows, we were strolling along when something caught our attention. There was an unusual number of black inmates and white inmates on the yard. They were in groups of about ten each. The vibe in the air was cold—and not just from the weather. We decided not to walk past them, and just posted up against the wall facing both large groups. Sure enough, they kicked it off! A full-blown race riot. We weren't in a position to run from it, so we got down on the ground the second it started. From where we lay, we saw men getting stabbed, beat, and finally shot by the CO in the tower.

After the smoke from the pepper gas canisters cleared, Spider and I were escorted back to our building, unharmed. It reminded me of the movie *Braveheart,* the scene where the two masses run toward each other with weapons, and the bloodiest feud unfolds. It's one thing to see it on TV or even a big movie screen, but when it's ten feet in front of you, it's something else altogether—and a lot more memorable, unfortunately.

RAMEN GOULASH

INGREDIENTS

2 packs beef flavor Ramen
1½ cups boiling water
1½ cups or ¾ pound beef chunks (about 11 ounces)
½ cup chopped cooked potatoes
½ cup chopped celery
½ cup chopped onion
2 jalapeño chiles, chopped
2 tablespoons mayonnaise

NOTE: I've been known to double the mayonnaise if I have it handy.

1. Crush the Ramen in the wrappers and empty into a bowl. Set aside the seasoning packets.
2. Add the water, cover, and let sit for 8 minutes.
3. Drain off excess water.
4. Mix the roast beef, potatoes, celery, onion, and jalapeños in a large microwavable bowl. Add a little water to moisten—about 2 tablespoons.
5. Cover and microwave for about 5 minutes, until hot.
6. Add the Ramen and mayonnaise. Mix well.

Romeo
{FROM *ALL SAINTS DAY*}
Addresses the Court

BY TROY DUFFY

I'm sitting in the courtroom facing my imminent demise, while the loud shrieks of "You killed my husband! Now his children will grow up with no daddy," etc., etc. ring in my ears. These are the voices of the family members of the men I had killed. I feel in some way betrayed. Don't they know what these animals they called father or husband were about? All these men were scum, the scum of this very earth! But I had been charged with three murder counts!

Then the judge gives me four f'ing minutes to respond before he sentences me on three counts of murder in the first! I'm like, "Really, Judge?!!" I'm thinking, *Oh hell naaah!* So I stand to respectfully retort.

"Your Honor, three? Just three? I was on Donkey Kong that day, it *had*

to be more than three, had to be. I demand a recount!"

I also addressed the gallery. "As for your husbands, fathers, and sons, apparently neither this court nor the media asked the following rather obvious questions. What were they *all* doing in those woods, armed to the teeth, with twenty other douches assaulting a house filled with people who kill known criminals for a living? Now, granted I'm aware that I was fresh in the game. I get it. I totally get it. I'm a nobody. But those other three? My associates? Whooo, all they did was kill assholes, all day every day. Seriously, they're like the holy trinity of asshole killers! Now, during the discovery process, I was provided the criminal histories of your husbands, fathers, and sons . . ."

At this point my lawyer rudely interrupts me and whispers in my ear, "I gave those to you confidentially, wasn't supposed to, blah blah blah . . ." To which I say, "WTF?! You were a shitty lawyer anyways. I hope you get in trouble. And Judge, if you need me to testify against this douche bag, no problem! Back to biz!"

So I turn to the gallery to perform my well-thought-out last hurrah speech, looking each person in the eyes. "Your husband was a rapist. Your father was a murdering rapist, and your son was a drug-dealing murderer who, to his credit, wasn't much for rape. Guess he really stood up to the peer pressure. But let's talk big picture. If there is any justice in the next world, your husbands, fathers, and sons are spending their days being force-fed demon cocks in hell and capping off every evening with a good old-fashioned ass raping from Satan himself. Well, except the lone nonrapist. Let's hope the Prince of Darkness rolls with the 'punishment fits the crime' crowd."

Then out of the corner of my eye, I catch this little girl, and my heart bleeds. "My only regret here is you, dear. I think in the years to come you are going to look into this and come down to my side, especially once you realize how your own family pimped you out to the media. For you, I just have sort of a, a, like a very soft 'fuck you.' Enough to let you know where I sat, ya' know? But not enough to . . ." Then she starts wailing.

I can't take it, so I turn to the judge. "Well, shit. Sorry. Judge, go ahead and throw the book. You know you want to."

The judge can't wait to sentence me, but then I realize I still have some time on the clock!

"HANG ON! Still got some time, and I'd just like to say . . . prison: looking forward to it. Haven't seen the 'family' in a while; besides, it's time to check in. Back to three hots and a cot and mandatory workouts. Could use a little more ink, too. Shit, ain't nothing changed but the time and the weather! Looking forward to cooking up my old Ramen spread with the fellows!"

TROY DUFFY Is a director, screenwriter, and musician. He directed *The Boondock Saints* and *The Boondock Saints II: All Saints Day*. This monologue imagines a scene in which Romeo from *Boondock II*, played by Clifton Collins Jr. as a ferocious underdog, addresses the court. He is on trial for murder after a barrage of bullets ended in a bloodbath that left several mobsters dead.

ROMEO'S "RAMEN CON PESCADO"

INGREDIENTS

1 pack chili flavor Ramen
1 cup boiling water
1½ cans (about 4 ounces each) mackerel, drained
1 can (3 to 4 ounces) sardines in hot sauce
1 can (3 to 4 ounces) smoked oysters, drained
2 tablespoons mayonnaise

1. Crush the Ramen in the wrapper and empty into a bowl. Set aside the seasoning packet.
2. Add the water, cover, and let sit for about 8 minutes.
3. Drain off excess water.
4. Add the seasoning, mackerel, sardines, oysters, and mayonnaise. Mix well.

No Hershey Squirts Here

When a federal inmate gets transferred to another prison, it's usually by air or bus. If it's by air, it's con-air. Do not eat or drink the night before a transfer of any kind. When you are handcuffed, shackled from waist and ankles, it is very difficult to use the restroom. And the guards don't really care how difficult it might be. I learned from the accidents of others that it's better to stay prepared for what's ahead. No matter how hungry I get or how weak I feel, I'd rather have an empty stomach than a full load.

A few days before you transfer, try a meal like this one. You'll have energy to spare, even after you've eliminated most of the meal.

RAMEN POT ROAST

INGREDIENTS

2 packs beef flavor Ramen
3 cups water
½ cup chopped carrots
½ cup chopped cooked potatoes
½ cup chopped celery
½ cup chopped green beans
½ cup beef broth
3 tablespoons soy sauce
½ cup cooked beef chunks

1. Crush the Ramen in the wrappers and empty into a large microwavable bowl. Add the seasoning.
2. Add the water, carrots, potatoes, celery, green beans, beef broth, soy sauce, and beef. Mix well.
3. Cover and microwave for 8 to 10 minutes, until hot.

Preparing for Battle at the Conjugal Visit

BY JACOB VARGAS

A lot of people ask me how I got to be known as the "Aztec Warrior." It all started when I was doing a stretch at Tracy. I hated doing time, eh. I got claustrophobia and shit, eh. I don't like locked doors! No more locked doors! Damn where was I? Oh yeah. So I was locked up and there was this female prison guard who kept flirting with me and shit. She told me she wanted to see my mini me. I must admit I was a bit nervous. It had been a long time since I'd done it with an actual woman. So my cellmate Lil Puppet (every Vato Loco knows a Lil Puppet) schooled me on a secret Ramen recipe that is guaranteed to get your lil soldier to attack and take no prisoners! It was called Ramen-Agra. Let me tell you this shit worked, eh! I took care of business and then some. I gave new meaning to the term "penal system"! She called me her Aztec Warrior. Ramen-Agra is great to eat right before a conjugal visit. Your lady will keep coming back for more. It will also keep her from running into Sancho's arms while you're locked up. If you're freaky and want to make it extra pungent, add a little oyster sauce. Just make sure your lady isn't allergic to seafood, if you know what I mean. Also make sure your cellmate doesn't eat too much of it or *you* might have to sleep with one eye open.

JACOB VARGAS is an actor who has appeared in several films, notably *Traffic* and *Jarhead*. He is perhaps most identified with his role as Joker in the film *Next Friday*. Vargas wrote this piece as Joker, taking his life a step beyond the movie. This is Joker telling the story of his time behind bars.

INGREDIENTS

1 pack shrimp flavor Ramen
1 cup boiling water
3 cans (about 3 ounces each) smoked oysters
1½ cans (about 4 ounces) mackerel
2 cans (3 ounces each) smoked baby clams
2 jalapeño chiles, chopped
Hot sauce

1. Crush the Ramen in the wrapper and empty into a bowl with seasoning from the packet.
2. Add the boiling water, cover, and let sit for 8 minutes.
3. Add the oysters, mackerel, baby clams, and jalapeños. Mix well.
4. Add hot sauce to taste.

AN EYE FOR AN ONION

Sometimes the inmate-on-inmate beatings you see in prison are for reasons that could make you laugh if they weren't ultimately so tragic. I watched a guy get beaten so badly he lost his eye. He was caught red-handed stealing onions that a bunch of other inmates had smuggled in. He was beaten with a weapon known as the "lock in the sock." This is a heavy iron padlock concealed inside a tube sock. The sock is knotted, and when it is swung quickly, making contact with soft parts of the body, it will cause severe damage, sometimes death.

One man loses an eye, another gets years added to his sentence. For vegetables! The guys who had been stolen from may have wanted to forget it, and say it's just not worth it, but there was no option. It's the convict code, the law of the land. Fight, and you spend longer in prison; walk away, and your life in prison is made even harder because you're an easy mark. You're stuck either way.

RAMEN CHINGA SOUP

INGREDIENTS

1 pack chili flavor Ramen
¾ cup boiling water
¾ cup crumbled cooked hamburger
¾ cup chopped cooked chicken breast
½ red onion, chopped
1 jalapeño chile, chopped
½ bag (2-ounce bag) pork skins or rinds
3 tablespoons strawberry jelly
3 tablespoons soy sauce

1. Crush the Ramen in the wrapper and empty into a bowl. Set aside the seasoning packet.
2. Add the water, cover, and let sit for 8 minutes.
3. Mix the hamburger, chicken, seasoning, onion, jalapeño, pork skins, jelly, and soy sauce in a large microwavable bowl.
4. Cover and microwave for about 5 minutes. Stir, re-cover, and microwave for 5 minutes more, until hot.
5. Add the Ramen. Mix well.

ROTTEN PIG

Gustavo "Goose" Alvarez

I was in my mid-thirties when I joined a recovery program at the California Correctional Institution in Tehachapi. I was tired of hearing the same bullshit in my life. I knew I had issues with my temper, but I didn't feel like there was anything I could do about it. Until my recovery counselor told me a story that I continue to share with anyone who seems to need it. This is how I remember hearing it.

There was a village in Africa that was suffering from a mysterious disease. It was killing the animals, the elders, the kids—just everyone. A group of scientists came to investigate. They found that the drinking water from the local river was contaminated with a deadly bacteria. They went to find the source of the water. It turns out it was coming from a mountain range where there was a huge pool of fresh water from melted mountain snow. The researchers tested that pool of water and found it worse than the actual river water! So they had a diving team go to the bottom of the pool to see what was causing this deadly bacteria. At the bottom of the pool they found a huge wild boar stuck at the opening where all the fresh water flowed into the river and down to the village. All the water was being filtered through this rotten pig, which caused the deadly bacteria to flow all the way down the river and infect everyone. Once the pig was pulled out, the fresh water coursed through and everyone was able to live healthy, normal lives.

I didn't understand what this

story had to do with my anger problems until my counselor asked me some questions. We ended up talking about one of my childhood friends. He was a crime partner I thought I could trust. When he had a chance to snitch and go free, that's exactly what he did. He pointed a finger and gave up all the evidence to find me guilty and sentenced to ten years. We had been best friends, and I never thought this could happen. I buried this anger and betrayal deep down, but it was affecting me in ways I couldn't even imagine. When there was a snitch on the prison yard, I would volunteer to "handle him," as we'd say. My trust issues were ruining my relationships with everyone. Having a short fuse didn't help.

When I finally came to terms with all this and realized my old friend was the rotten pig affecting me and my "village," I was told to do what seemed impossible: forgive him. You can imagine my anger when I heard this. After a couple of months, I finally stepped up to face it. Not many convicts agree with the idea of forgiveness, but I was tired and just needed some change in my life. So I forgave him. I even sent him a letter explaining how I had been feeling all these years and told him not to worry. Our feud was over and I did not hold him responsible anymore. He responded, and from his letter it was clear he'd been carrying the heavy weight of what he had done. His apology was sincere, and I accepted it. Things have turned out so much better.

When you let stuff go, it's like being able to take a deep breath for the first time. Check yourself. Who knows what rotten pig you may be dealing with and how it might affect others in your life. I have found that life is just too short for grudges.

✦ 3 ✦

Gen Pop

"GEN POP" MEANS "GENERAL POPULATION." IT REFERS TO PRISONERS WHO ARE ON THE MAIN LINE—WHERE YOU ARE NOT CONFINED TO A CELL ALL DAY OR LIMITED TO ONLY CERTAIN INGREDIENTS. THESE RECIPES CAN FEED MORE THAN TWO—SOMETHING WE CALL A SPREAD. BEING IN GEN POP—WITH ITS ACCESS TO BOILING WATER AND OCCASIONAL FRESH INGREDIENTS—HAS ITS PERKS, INCLUDING WEEKEND POTLUCKS, BIRTHDAY SPREADS, AND PAROLE PARTIES.

The Wheels on the Bus

The Gray Goose was the bus that took us on the five-hour journey from the county jail to the California State Prison in Corcoran. If you were on it, it meant you'd be spending some serious time at Corcoran. The ride began at dawn, and most of the inmates were too tired to talk or notice anything around them as the bus climbed the Grapevine—the interstate that runs from the border of Mexico up north along the length of California. I knew I wouldn't be traveling south on this road for years to come. Regret jangled in my mind like the shackles on my wrists and ankles.

My first day in, some homies from West Los Angeles invited me to share a meal. Outside that prison, I may have looked tough, but inside those walls—and inside me—I was a scared kid. The invitation felt like a lifeline. Those three guys shared stories, gave me advice, and made me feel less afraid.

Sharing food helps weed out the good from the bad—even in prison. Guys who have seen people come and go for years know how to size you up—or as they put it, "run a make on you." They judge who you are, what you represent, and if you can be a trustworthy member of the group. In most cases, they already know who you are before you step off the bus. If you're no good, you wouldn't warrant eye contact, much less a shared meal. I always carried my court transcripts. They provided not only legal confirmation of your case, but proof that you were "good," as we'd put it. Not a pedophile, not a rapist, not a punk. I passed the test by the guys from West L.A. and was invited to share their meal of cheesy tacos. After the third taco, my new life in Corcoran began.

CHEESY MEAT TACOS

INGREDIENTS

3 summer sausages (about 9 ounces each), chopped, or 3 cans (9 ounces each) Vienna sausage, drained and chopped

1 bag (about 4 ounces) pork skins or rinds

5 tablespoons strawberry jelly

¾ cup soy sauce

1 tablespoon garlic powder

Pinch of crushed red pepper

½ onion, chopped

1 jalapeño chile, chopped

2 cups shredded cheese

4 to 6 corn tortillas

1. Mix the sausages, pork skins, jelly, soy sauce, garlic powder, red pepper, onion, and jalapeño in a large microwavable bowl.
2. Cover and microwave for 5 minutes.
3. Mix well, adding the cheese, re-cover, and microwave for 5 minutes more.
4. Microwave the tortillas for 30 seconds or heat on a stovetop griddle.
5. Spread the cheesy meat on the tortillas, fold, and eat while hot.

Looks Can Be Deceiving

When I first met the old guy, I had the impression that he was in for something petty like a D.U.I. or drug use. But this "harmless" old guy had been down for about thirty-two years by then. He stood about five-foot-five, salt-and-pepper hair, and had a huge mustache. At that time he was in his early sixties and in better shape than some twenty-year-olds. He was highly respected and feared by everyone. He was a well-known hit man with a strong affiliation to the Mexican mafia. He always struck me as wise and humble. I was lucky to share a few conversations with him. Once, I asked him about the people he'd killed. After a brief silence where I feared I'd been out of line, he smiled sadly and said, "There were many, but none haunts me more than my first." At that moment I felt it best to change the subject. It seemed to me after all these years, he was still dealing with what he had done for a "living."

Despite his past, I never saw him lose his temper or get into an altercation with anyone. In fact, he was always very giving and every Saturday afternoon he would make these very spicy burritos and share some of his stories about his past. I felt like I was eating at a Mexican restaurant while watching an old gangster movie.

HIT MAN BURRITOS

INGREDIENTS

2 packs beef flavor Ramen

2½ cups boiling water

1 cup or pouch (about 6 ounces) whole kernel corn

1 pouch (about 8 ounces) microwavable pinto beans and rice

1½ cups seasoned beef crumbles or seasoned crumbled cooked ground beef

6 tablespoons spicy nacho cheese sauce

6 flour tortillas

NOTE: Many brands make a 5- to 6-ounce pouch of beef crumbles; you'll need two pouches.

1. Crush the Ramen in the wrappers and empty into a bowl. Set aside one seasoning packet and save the other for another use.
2. Add the water, cover, and let sit for about 8 minutes. Drain off excess water. Cover to keep warm.
3. Prepare the corn and the beans and rice as directed on the packages.
4. Microwave the beef crumbles in a large bowl for 3 to 5 minutes, until hot.
5. Add the corn, beans and rice, seasoning, and Ramen. Mix well.
6. Microwave the cheese sauce for about a minute, until hot and spreadable.
7. Spread a large spoonful of the beef mixture on a tortilla.
8. Drizzle 1 tablespoon of the cheese sauce over the beef mixture. Wrap and eat.
9. Repeat until the tortillas, beef mixture, and cheese are gone.

Charlie

When I was in the California State Prison in Corcoran, I was getting a medical checkup, so they placed me in a holding cell by myself. The cell must have been right next to a landing pad, because on the day I was there, the sound of a helicopter was loud and clear. I had a little daydream, imagining the helicopter was for me, to fly my ass out of there. Sadly, I was snapped out of my dream by all kinds of commotion between officers and medical staff. I saw a huge correctional officer escorting a prisoner who must have come from the helicopter. As they got closer, the officers yelled out, "Face the wall!" as they walked the inmate past my cell. My curiosity got the best of me, and I caught a glimpse of the inmate they were escorting. I got quite a beat down for disobeying, but it was worth it to see Charles Manson eye to eye.

Manson's story is notorious and became the subject of several films and documentaries. He led what became known as the Manson Family, a quasi commune in the California desert in the late 1960s. He is in prison for life on several counts of murder. He looked like one crazy guy, all right.

RAMEN BEAN DIP

INGREDIENTS

1 pack chili flavor Ramen
1 cup boiling water
1 can (15 to 16 ounces) refried beans
1 can (14 to 16 ounces) hot chili beans
1 jalapeño chile, chopped
½ cup shredded cheese

1. Crush the Ramen in the wrapper and empty into a bowl. Set aside the seasoning packet.
2. Add the water, cover, and let sit for 8 minutes.
3. Drain off excess water.
4. Add the seasoning. Mix well.
5. Mix the refried beans, chili beans, and jalapeño in a large microwavable bowl.
6. Add the Ramen and cheese and stir.
7. Cover and microwave for 5 minutes, until hot.

UNCONTROLLABLE TEMPER

One of the many things that a prisoner needs to check at the door is his temper. There was an old friend of mine we called Short Dog, who'd been down almost five years for possession of a gun. We met on the handball court—he was one of the best players on the yard. He must have been about five feet tall and had quite a Napoleon complex. Every time he'd play handball he attracted a lot of attention. He had unbelievable speed—and the way he'd dive for the ball was like nothing we'd seen before. Some homies would clown around with him and yell, "*Andale, andale, arriba!*" a reference to Speedy Gonzalez, the little Mexican mouse cartoon character. He would get mad and allow his temper to get the best of him, getting into scuffles with other homies.

One day we were discussing our plans for when we got out. He was paroling in three months and talked about opening his own auto shop and starting a family. He was so excited to get this life started. The following day at the handball court, I noticed one of the yard officers watching the game. The officer had a reputation of being a real dick. By the time I arrived, he'd clearly been harassing Short Dog for a while. I could see it was getting to him, and he was feeling humiliated in front of all the guys. It got really heated and before we could intervene, Short Dog knocked the cop out cold. Three months to parole turned into ten years for assault on an officer. What a waste.

SPICY SHRIMP SPREAD

INGREDIENTS

2 packs lime shrimp flavor Ramen
1 can (6 to 7 ounces) baby shrimp, drained
¾ cup spicy dried shrimp (about ½ pound)
½ red onion, chopped
1 jalapeño chile, chopped
1½ cups boiling water
Hot sauce

1. Crush the Ramen in the wrappers and empty into a bowl. Add the seasoning.
2. Add the baby shrimp, dried shrimp, onion, and jalapeño. Add the water.
3. Add hot sauce to taste, stir well, cover, and let sit for about 8 minutes.

Maybe Tomorrow, Maybe Not

Just after dinner one night, I decided to make a cup of coffee to take outside for night yard. That's the time you get to hang out with the homies, walking the yard with a nice cup of coffee, shooting the shit. I was rushing out to the yard so as not to miss my time there, and I spilled my coffee right in front of the control booth and gun tower. I obviously couldn't just leave the mess, so I went to grab the cellblock mop that was next to the control booth. Just as I was about to fill the bucket with water at the sink, a Spanish guy asked me if he could go first just to rinse his cup off. I let him go ahead as I waved to the officer in the tower to open my cell again. I knew I wasn't going to make it out to yard in time so I figured I'd clean my cell.

As I was walking toward my cell, all of a sudden I heard the telltale sound. *Pop. Pop.* "GET DOWN!" yelled the officer, gun in hand. The officer in the tower shot directly toward the shower, which opened out onto the yard. Two African American inmates were fighting in there, butt naked. When the guys separated and lay down as directed, I could hear the cries from the Spanish guy: "*Dios mio!*" He had been shot by accident, just trying to rinse out his coffee cup. That bullet could have been mine. After that, I stopped believing tomorrow was guaranteed.

CHICKEN RAMEN TOSTADAS

INGREDIENTS

1 pack chicken flavor Ramen
1 cup boiling water
½ cup shredded cooked chicken breast
1 can (15 to 16 ounces) refried beans
½ onion, chopped
1 jalapeño chile, chopped
1 tomato, chopped
4 tostadas
½ cup shredded lettuce

1. Crush the Ramen in the wrapper and empty into a bowl. Set aside the seasoning packet.
2. Add the water, cover, and let sit for 8 minutes.
3. Drain off excess water.
4. Mix the chicken, refried beans, seasoning, onion, jalapeño, and tomato in a microwavable bowl.
5. Cover and microwave for about 5 minutes, until hot.
6. Add the Ramen. Mix well.
7. Spread the mixture on the tostadas and add a good handful of lettuce.

Movie Night

Movie night in prison was usually a big deal. We didn't get to watch any new or R-rated movies, but they did bring in a big old projector and showed movies on a huge screen in the chow hall. It kind of made it feel like you were actually *at* the movies.

One movie night involved some famous people—but not actors. A vicious hit was carried out by members of the L.A. gang, the Crips. There was a guy in the prison who was a member of the rival group—the notorious Bloods. You could tell this was a planned hit by the precise mechanics of the execution. The projector was set up, and the guys were in a pretty good mood. But just as the lights went out and the movie began, the soundtrack kicked in and got loud. That was the cue. Right next to me, there was a sudden movement and I saw the guy I knew to be a Crip put his hand over the Blood's mouth as he simultaneously sliced his neck with one smooth, quick motion. Before the lights came on, the assassin was out of the chow hall, nowhere to be seen. That night, nothing that happened on the screen matched the drama around us.

JAILHOUSE POPCORN

INGREDIENTS

1 pack chili flavor Ramen

NOTE: Chili flavor Ramen is best for this recipe. Other flavors just don't do it.

1. Crush the Ramen in the wrapper.
2. Open the wrapper on one end only and take out the seasoning packet.
3. Sprinkle the seasoning into the crushed Ramen, close the bag, and shake until the seasoning is distributed.

THE CELLMATE CHALLENGE

The two essentials to cell living are mutual respect and common courtesy. When two men are living in a cell the size of a small restroom, both of these things are a matter of life and death. There are rules, and sometimes new cellmates need to be informed. For example, two inmates can't walk around the cell at the same time, so there is a "one up, one down" program. This means one inmate is up and doing whatever he needs to do—restroom, brush teeth, cook, birdbath, and even exercise—while the other waits on the bed, staying out of the way. Also, if your cellmate is asleep you should have the courtesy of not making too much noise. I've been in prisons where inmates kill their cellmates over stuff that wouldn't matter outside.

One of the best cellmates I had was a lifer homie named Rascal. We got along so well that lockdowns weren't even that bad. He was a few years older and a real clown. He was so upbeat that you couldn't tell he was facing twenty-five to life. I don't think there was a day this homie didn't make me laugh, and he always respected my space.

RASCAL'S RAMEN PASTRAMI

INGREDIENTS

2 packs chili flavor Ramen
1½ cups boiling water
1 pouch (6 ounces) pastrami
½ onion, sliced into half-moons
1 jalapeño chile, sliced into wheels
2 tablespoons soy sauce (about 1 ounce)
Mustard
1 hoagie or hero roll, split open
Hot pickle wheels

1. Crush the Ramen in the wrappers and empty into a bowl. Set aside the seasoning packets.
2. Add the water, cover, and let sit for 8 minutes.
3. Drain off excess water.
4. Combine the pastrami, onion, jalapeño, and soy sauce in a large microwavable bowl.
5. Cover and microwave for 5 minutes, or until hot.
6. Add the Ramen and seasonings. Mix well.
7. Spread mustard in the roll. Add the pastrami mixture and pickle wheels.

EXPRESS MAIL

When an important and confidential message needs to travel from prison to prison, in most cases we'll carry a note, wrapped in plastic, in a place where the sun never shines. In most cases, the note is written in detail and made as compact as possible. It could be as long as half a page, and is folded and rolled into the size of an enema. It's wrapped several times with plastic from the sack lunch. If you are the person transferring the note, you prepare your "suitcase," if you will, by making sure it is completely empty. You lather the plastic-wrapped message with hair grease and just before you hear the officers walking toward your cell with the handcuffs and shackles for your waist and legs, you insert the note into your suitcase. You'll be glad you didn't eat anything the night before.

Once you arrive at your destination, you will get strip-searched, and cavity-searched as well. It's rare for the officer to see the note you've "keistered," and once this search is over, you'll be put inside a holding cell. At this point, you have to sit on the toilet and shit the note out. Once you've cleaned the item thoroughly, it's ready for delivery. The addressee will be looking for you and ready to receive instructions.

RAMEN TRAIL MIX

INGREDIENTS

1 pack chili flavor Ramen
Heaping ½ cup raisins (4 ounces)
1 cup salted peanuts (about 4 ounces)
½ cup chopped pitted dates (4 ounces)
Heaping ½ cup dried banana chips (4 ounces)

1. Crush the Ramen in the wrapper and empty into a large bowl.
2. Add half of the seasoning.
3. Add the raisins, peanuts, dates, and banana chips. Mix well.

Road Dog

People doing hard time don't really trust anyone. But every once in a while, you'll meet someone you connect with. Sometimes it's a homeboy you are doing time with, or one you meet behind bars. When the bond is made inside, it's stronger than it might be outside. You become brothers fast, looking after each other. In prison, the name for your closest friend and ally is your "road dog."

But the politics of prison override everything—even that bond. Once I was asked to do the unthinkable—kill my road dog. I was given an order from the Mexican shot caller to stab my friend. Before he was arrested, he allegedly shot his gun into a crowd of rival gang members and struck a young girl. Bad luck all around—she was the daughter of a Mexican mafia member. The order came specifically to me. Stabbing my friend didn't seem right, but prison has its own rules and if you don't follow them, you die. It's that simple.

So we set it up. It was Saturday, and our favorite Spanish show, *Caliente,* was on—pretty girls dancing in bikinis. We were all enjoying the show, drinking coffee together. As I gave the signal to the four guys who were the distraction, they walked to the opposite side of the cellblock and began horsing around. The moment the gunner officer in the tower began to walk toward them, my two guys and I pulled out our shanks and began the assault. Once the victim was curled up in a fetal position, we threw the shanks in the nearby trash cans and dispersed in opposite directions. I was able to get to a shower area, take off most of my clothes, and get into the stall. When the victim was discovered, the officers shouted to get down, to the accompanying sound of guns being cocked. I lay in my boxer shorts near the showers and watched the medics and several officers arrive. The other two assailants were apprehended due to the blood on their clothing.

Afterward, we were locked down for a couple of months. We found out the victim survived and was in the local hospital pending transfer to another prison. Once we got off lockdown, the shot caller acknowledged the deed done. But I felt like shit about it. Still do.

RAMEN CHIPS

INGREDIENTS

2 packs chili flavor Ramen
½ cup corn chips
½ cup tortilla chips
½ cup potato chips
½ cup pork skins or rinds
Hot sauce

1. Crush the Ramen in the wrappers and empty into a large bowl.
2. Sprinkle one of the seasonings over the Ramen. Save the other for another use.
3. Add the corn chips, tortilla chips, potato chips, pork skins, and hot sauce to taste. Mix well.

LIFELINES

BY CLARENCE J. "CLANCY" BROWN III

It seems like I've been working in jails for my entire adult life. From Joliet to Rahway; Soledad to Angola; St. Charles, Illinois, to L.A. County; Mansfield, Ohio, to Feliciana Parish, Louisiana. I've even worked in imaginary prisons in Maine and in outer space. Here's what I know for sure: they all suck. Even in my privileged visits as an observer, student, or actor, the overwhelming vibe in these places is of souls suppressed, lives in limbo, injustice, anger, and fear. There are men there who should be in prison, but not as many as you'd think. Many just fucked up once or twice. Most pled-out in a system stacked against them, or that they couldn't afford to participate in, so the system chucks them. It takes their liberty—the essential element of their humanity—and expects them to self-correct or at least be a "dude" and abide. Some manage. Some can't. Prisons are places where humanity is withheld, suspended; and the struggle to recover or maintain or assert humanity pulses through every institution I've ever visited.

As far as I can tell, there are two lifelines to one's humanity, even as it is being systematically assaulted. The first is music. In my opinion, the most satisfying moment in *The Shawshank Redemption* is when Andy Dufresne locks himself in the room with the PA system and plays Mozart throughout the prison. The other is food. Eating a meal, no matter how simple, is the essential element of liberty. A moment to savor, be sated, and get refueled. The first thing released inmates look forward to is a meal. Whether it's from Mickey D or from momma, it means you've survived, you're still human. There is always food in a prison movie. It's where men can talk, where plots are hatched, where alliances are forged, where peace is kept, and, for dramatic purposes, violated. It is as close to normal society as an inmate is routinely allowed to participate in. So eat. Simply. Safely. Consciously. It connects you to your humanity.

CLARENCE J. "CLANCY" BROWN III is a film, television, and voice actor. He played Captain Byron Hadley in *The Shawshank Redemption.*

SHAWSHANK SPREAD

INGREDIENTS

1 pack beef flavor Ramen
1 cup boiling water
¼ pound sliced ham, chopped
¼ pound sliced turkey, chopped
½ white onion, chopped
2 jalapeño chiles, chopped
¼ teaspoon garlic powder
½ cup mayonnaise

1. Crush the Ramen in the wrapper and empty into a large bowl. Set aside the seasoning packet.
2. Add the water, cover, and let sit for 8 minutes.
3. Drain off excess water.
4. Mix the ham, turkey, onion, jalapeños, garlic, and mayonnaise in a separate, very large bowl.
5. Add the Ramen and seasoning. Mix well.

20/20 HINDSIGHT

When I was in my thirties, I felt it was my responsibility to try to make a change in a younger inmate's life. I was making these nachos when two youngsters, about nineteen years old, came over to see what I was doing. They considered themselves hardcore, so I knew I had to win them over before the schooling could begin. They were just kids, but their crimes where heavy. Out in the streets of Mexico they were called *sicarios,* which means "hit men." But inside these walls, they were just another pair of numbers. They weren't that bad—just terribly misguided. Without an education or money, it's easy to get brainwashed into a life of violence, believing you'll be protected within it. I saw my younger self in them. I wanted to give them the eyes to change the way they looked at things, so that the things they looked at would change.

We started meeting just to talk and shoot the shit. After months of this, I started to talk about more serious stuff—the kind of stuff I wish I'd known when I was their age. After a while, I could see my stories and ideas were affecting their way of thinking. They got involved with the school program, became regulars at the library, began talking differently. One of them even began to make amends with his family. I got to see the darkness in their eyes being replaced by hope before our friendship was forced to end.

The riots were out of control; inmates were being separated and shipped off to different prisons. Even though they had long prison terms ahead of them, I knew they were on a road to improving their lives for when they would get out.

CARNE ASADA NACHOS

INGREDIENTS

3 cups or 3 bags (1 ounce each) tortilla chips

1½ cups charbroiled steak strips
(also sold as fajita strips or carne asada strips)

1 cup microwavable cheese spread

Pickled jalapeño wheels

1. Spread the tortilla chips evenly on a plate.
2. Lay the steak strips over the chips.
3. Microwave the cheese for about 3 minutes, until pourable.
4. Pour the cheese over the steak and chips.
5. Top with the jalapeño wheels.

Lifesaving Coffee

Once, at the L.A. County jail, I saw a man lying on the floor, shivering and sweating like crazy. You could tell he was a big-time addict by looking at his arms. Another inmate brought him this special drink—the Belushi. About 30 minutes later, after finishing it, he was calm and composed enough to walk over and thank the man.

I asked the lifesaving coffee maker why he called it a Belushi. He explained that John Belushi was a great comedian who died of a drug overdose. I guess having a sanity-saving, sugar-filled coffee drink named after you isn't a bad way to be remembered. It's loaded with sugar and helps with the symptoms of heroin detoxing.

THE BELUSHI

INGREDIENTS

1 tablespoon instant coffee granules
(Taster's Choice or Folgers works best)

1 tablespoon sugar

5 tablespoons French vanilla flavor creamer

1 cup boiling water

½ full-size (52-gram) or 1 miniature Milky Way bar

1. Place the coffee in a large mug. Add the sugar and creamer. Add the water and stir well.
2. Add the Milky Way.
3. Drink immediately, while the candy bar melts.

PRISON COLD

The prison head cold affects everyone and there's no cure for it but freedom. It comes from living in a place where hygiene is nonexistent and the temperature is kept below normal all the time. Sometimes it feels like you're sleeping in a refrigerator. The control booth officer decides the temperature. You can complain as much as you want, but a convict's personal comfort is not a priority. In winter we're freezing our balls off, and in summer they're stuck on our sweaty thighs. In winter, when cold air would blast through the vents, we'd use toilet paper cardboard to plug the holes in the vent. If everyone on the cell row—or tier—did this, it would cause the weakest vent covers to blow off. It would look like a tornado hit the cell.

THE TEA SETUP

INGREDIENTS

1 tea bag (any kind)
A few nickel-size pieces orange peel
3 cough drops (any flavor, but honey is best)
1 tablespoon sugar
1½ cups boiling water
2 tablespoons honey

1. Put the tea bag, orange peel, cough drops, and sugar in a mug big enough to hold them all easily.
2. Pour in the water, add the honey, and stir.
3. Let steep for about 4 minutes.
4. Stir again, then remove the tea bag.
5. Drink while it's hot—although it's not bad cold, either.

A BOND BETWEEN "ENEMIES"

After serving nearly a year at Corcoran, my appeal was being granted and I was returning to the L.A. County jail. As I approached my housing cell where I would await court on the appeal, I saw that I was being placed in a four-man cell. This wasn't the problem. With a quick glance, I took in a white guy bunked with a Mexican on one side. On the other side, I locked eyes with a black guy who immediately stood up into an aggressive stance. *That* was the problem. "Hell no, I'm not celling with this dude." My words fell upon the deputy's deaf ears. A homie in another cell said, "Don't trip, bro, just deal with it for now and at dinner I'll explain." When dinner was called a little while later, I kicked back and waited for my cellmates to leave. That's when the homies on the tier gave me a shank and told me to carry it with me at all times due to the racial tensions.

When I returned from dinner, everyone was pretty much quiet, minding their own business. Then the white dude in the cell asked if we wanted to play Spades. He immediately picked his bunky, the Mexican, as his partner, saying they would play us. Me and the big guy looked at each other. "You play Spades, homie?" he said. I was a bit hesitant but because I was already in the cell, and packing, I said, "Sure." I introduced myself, and met Big Kev.

Well, the two of us must have won twenty games straight. It was like he could see my cards and knew exactly what I needed him to play. After what seemed like five hours of cards, our opponents fell asleep. Kev and I stayed up and got to talking. I found out he had just been sentenced to fifty to life. He was only nineteen years old. He also had enough commissary that he was able to cook us a fantastic Tuna Spread. We just ate, drank coffee, and chopped it up for hours. Finally, just before breakfast, we called it a night. I felt comfortable enough to take my boots off. He asked me if I was going to get up for breakfast. I said, "Nah, I'm tired from being up all night, I'm going to skip it."

Next thing I knew, I was jolted from a deep sleep by a yank on my leg through the cell bars. Looking up, I saw it was Big Kev—and he was running off. A second later, two big black dudes ran in and started beating me. I reached under my pillow for my shank and started swinging until I stuck one of my assailants under his chin. When they realized I had a knife and had stuck one of them, they stepped back and ran off. I jumped off my bed, swollen, bleeding from my nose, and slammed my cell door shut. After the smoke cleared, I discovered a vicious riot had occurred in the breakfast mess hall while I was sleeping. I never saw Big Kev again, but I realized he had saved my life. Thanks for looking out for me, brother.

BIG KEV'S TUNA SPREAD

INGREDIENTS

2 packs Ramen (any flavor)
About 1 cup boiling water
½ cup mayonnaise
2 cans or pouches tuna (5 to 6 ounces each), drained
2 avocados, pitted, peeled, and chopped
1 cup shredded cheese (pepper Jack is best)

1. Crush and empty the Ramen into a large microwavable bowl and set the seasoning aside.
2. Add the water, cover, and microwave for about 5 minutes, until the noodles are soft.
3. Drain off excess water, if necessary.
4. Add the mayonnaise, seasoning, tuna, and avocado. Mix gently but well.
5. Top with the cheese.

ONLY THE STRONG SURVIVE

Looking at these recipes, you might think we're a bunch of big-belly pasta eaters and totally unhealthy. Not true. Being fit in prison is akin to having homies in prison. Without it, you're closer to dead.

Of all government-sponsored organizations, Navy Seals have the most rigorous workout of all. But let me tell you, the prison workouts I've done behind bars could make even a Navy Seal throw up. In a cell of no more than six by eight feet, we do four exercises regularly.

The Roman chair workout is done barefoot, using the toilet as a prop: Step up and down on the cover or rim of the toilet, alternating the lifting leg. Speed up as you progress. Do this for 30 minutes.

After a 5-minute break, go into frog squats: Squat with hands on the ground in front of your feet. Jump your legs back away from you, then jump them back in. Do twenty sets of forty squats, for a total of—that's right—800.

After another 5-minute break, start in on 1,000 pushups—twenty sets of fifty.

Enjoy another short break, then start in on 500 crunches.

This is just one of many routines that can be done in a cell. It can take a couple of hours to complete—or until you or your cellmate have had enough. Puking was a norm for the out-of-shape newbies.

But the real deal takes place out on the yard. That's where we go beyond military. I used to run eight to ten miles on the track, followed by 113 burpees. The "burpee" is a full-body exercise that's great for small indoor spaces, and even better outdoors where you can grunt in pain. The basic movement is performed in four steps, beginning from a standing position:

- Drop into a squat position with your hands on the ground.
- Kick your feet back, while keeping your arms straight.
- Immediately return your feet to the squat position.
- Jump up from the squat position.

When I was first attempting these exercises, I couldn't last through the entire workout. It took me a few months to build up the stamina. With more advanced homies giving me hell, and the added stress of doing time, I burned through all my frustrations until I was able to keep up. I've never been in the military, but I felt as though this was a type of boot camp. In prison it's the evolutionary rule—survival of the fittest.

OATMEAL SHAKEDOWN

INGREDIENTS

2 packs instant oatmeal (flavored or unflavored)
6 tablespoons honey
6 tablespoons peanut butter
1 cup crushed ice
2 teaspoons instant coffee granules
1 cup water

1. Empty the oatmeal into a large jar. (Use a jar with a lid, preferably an empty peanut butter jar. This will be your mixer and one of your serving containers.)
2. Add the honey, peanut butter, ice, coffee, and water.
3. Close the jar tightly and shake until it looks like a thick milkshake. This can be a workout for your arms. If you have access to a blender, you are clearly not in prison.

The Great Spread Controversy

BY FATHER GREG BOYLE OF HOMEBOY INDUSTRIES

It was the turn of the twenty-first century when the Great Spread Controversy erupted. Homeboy Industries had outgrown itself and was now in its third headquarters. Then, as now, it was the largest gang-intervention, rehab, and reentry program on the planet. Fifteen thousand folks had walked through our doors trying to reimagine life after gangs and prison. Enemies worked alongside one another in a variety of social enterprises from a bakery to a restaurant to a silk-screening factory. Trainees, all rivals, filled the headquarters, answering phones, processing people through tattoo removal, and facilitating the location of jobs through our employment services department.

The workers had to eat. They drew on the rare positive experiences of their lives in prison—and the idea for a communal spread was born. Every week two guys would go to the 99-cent store and shop for the feast. Ramen and a variety of Cup Noodles, jars of mayonnaise, cans of sardines, bags of beef jerky, flaming red hots. Homies would bring random items like a can of menudo or refried beans. All ingredients were included—none disparaged or deemed unsuitable.

The "chefs" would toss all this crap into a very large garbage bag. They'd fill it with the hottest tap water and then they'd wait for it to "blow up"—expand into its fully hydrated glory. This took until nearly noon. Then they'd shift the whole pregnant thing on its side and perform a "C-section," carefully drawing a knife across the guts of the bag to reveal the now cooked concoction. Twenty or so homies would grab their bowls and swoon at their bona fide definition of comfort food.

The controversy? Senior staff at Homeboy began to complain how time-consuming the whole ritual had become. Trainees would be milling in the kitchen all morning, adding newfound and always welcome ingredients. Or someone would need to race down to the 99-cent store to buy that extra can of jalapeños or that jar of salsa. No work got done. This seemed to annoy some people. I bowed to the pressure and officially halted the practice. The grumblers among the homies approached Father Mark, another Jesuit who worked at Homeboy, to advocate for its reinstatement.

"Spreads," he told me, standing in front of my desk, "are the Kingdom of God. They obliterate the illusion that we are separate." He went on like this, quite convincingly. I thought, *how can I say efficiency trumps* El Reino de Dios? I reversed my decision. The spreads were reinstated to much joy.

Spreads remind us that we belong to one another. The dollars get corralled, the Ramen and Cheetos get combined, the stuff magically blows up, and rivals who used to shoot at one another slurp this red mess into a newfound sense of belonging. Kinship in a garbage bag.

FATHER GREG BOYLE is founder of Homeboy Industries and author of *Tattoos on the Heart: The Power of Boundless Compassion*. He has received numerous humanitarian awards including the California Peace Prize.

KOINONIA RAMEN

FEEDS 15 TO 20

INGREDIENTS

10 packs Ramen (any flavor)
10 Cup Noodles (any flavor)
10 cans (5.5 ounces each) sardines, drained
5 bags (3 ounces each) beef jerky, chopped
10 bags (9 ounces each) Flamin' Cheetos
About 10 cups very hot water
4 jars (15 ounces each) mayonnaise
2 cans (26 ounces each) pickled jalapeño wheels, drained

NOTES:

- *Koinonia* is the Greek word for "fellowship."
- Use very hot tap water; boiling water may melt the bag.
- A 2-liter soda bottle holds 8½ cups, so you'll need about 1¼ bottles.

1. Crush the Ramen in the wrappers and empty into an extra-large, heavy-duty plastic bag. Add all the seasoning.
2. Add the Cup Noodles, sardines, beef jerky, and Cheetos. Mix well.
3. Add the very hot water until everything is submerged. Use more or less water as needed. Mix gently by jiggling the bag.
4. Carefully tie a knot in the bag top so it looks like a big water balloon. Set the bag on a towel on a clean surface.
5. Let it sit for 20 to 25 minutes. Open the bag; the Ramen should have fluffed up and there should be little to no water left.
6. Add the mayonnaise and jalapeños. Mix gently.
7. Serve immediately.

Run of Fives

BY DANNY TREJO

At San Quentin State Prison, we played a lot of dominos. One time I had a run of fives in my hand—four dominos, each with the five dots showing. When it was my turn to play, I was going to set the spin on my opponents, that is, turn the game and control it in my favor. There were a lot of spectators and this was a big money dominos game. Just as I was ready to make my move, there was a lot of commotion right behind me, and a guy fell to the ground. He'd been stabbed while watching us play. I guess he'd snitched on some guy years ago and was finally paying for it with his life. Well, he was stabbed so many times that he actually fell right onto our table.

Of course, everyone started to run away from the crime scene. When a hit goes down and you're in the area of the crime, chances are you'll be blamed for it. But I stayed where I was, yelling out, "Wait, let's finish this game; I got a run of fives!" In that moment, a good Mexican friend of mine, Tyrone, grabbed me from behind and pulled me away as I'm yelling, "Wait, wait! I had a run of fives!" Tyrone yelled at me, "*Puto*, what's wrong with you? That guy just got stuck!" and dragged me away from the bloody guy on the table.

I didn't realize what I was doing until I got back to my cell. Sitting there, I thought, *That guy had a mom, dad, brother, and I didn't think his life was as important as my run of fives. What is my life turning into? I mean, when we see an accident we think,* Oh my God, I hope no one's hurt. *But in here, I'm trying to push this guy off the domino table! WTF?*

So you learn ways to overcome, and you're glad for guys looking after you when you can't see trouble—even if it falls right on your table.

DANNY TREJO. Before Danny Trejo became known for playing the anti-hero in dozens of films and TV series, he was a drug counselor, often helping teenage kids. His first acting role came when he was called to a movie set to help a kid who had an addiction issue. He helped the kid and was cast in the film. Trejo has said, "Everything good that has ever happened to me has happened as a direct result of helping someone else."

TREJO'S RAMEN QUESADILLA

INGREDIENTS

2 packs chili flavor Ramen
1½ cups boiling water
1 tablespoon butter, softened
8 flour tortillas
½ cup shredded pepper Jack cheese

1. Crush the Ramen in the wrappers and empty into a bowl. Set aside the seasoning packets.
2. Add the water, cover, and let sit for 8 minutes.
3. Drain off excess water.
4. Add the seasoning. Mix well.
5. Heat an electric or stove-top griddle, or a large skillet.
6. When the griddle is hot, brush it with about 1 teaspoon of the butter. Place a tortilla on the griddle.
7. Sprinkle one quarter of the cheese on top of the tortilla and top with one quarter of the Ramen.
8. Cover with another tortilla and press down with a spatula to flatten it like a pancake.
9. After a few minutes, when the bottom is golden brown, use the spatula to flip it over. Let the other side cook until golden brown.
10. Repeat with the rest of the butter, tortillas, cheese, and Ramen.

Cell Locker Cooker

Back before microwaves were so common and cheap they could be in prison, we had cookers. They were homemade stoves created by using the steel shelf from your locker combined with a mini electric burner you'd make in metal or electronic repair shop.

To make the not-exactly-legal cooker, you'd sand the paint off the shelf and clean it. When you put the burner under it, the shelf would get hot enough to act like a griddle and you could make grilled cheese, fried eggs, you name it. Once, we got some pancake mix. Man, we gave IHOP a run for their money. We were making pancakes night and day. It got to the point that on the weekends, my cellmate and I started selling two fat pancakes for four Ramen. With a little butter smuggled back from chow, you'd have that awesome home cooking taste we missed so much. On the downside, cleaning the cooker was a pain in the ass. But definitely worth the trouble.

CHOCOLATE CHIP PANCAKES

FEEDS 2 OR 3
*CAN BE EASILY DOUBLED FOR MORE HOMIES

INGREDIENTS

1 cup all-purpose flour
2 tablespoons sugar
2 tablespoons baking powder
½ teaspoon salt
1 large egg, lightly beaten
2 tablespoons butter, melted
¼ cup milk
5 Hershey's Kisses, chopped
Vegetable oil or more butter, for the cooker

NOTE: Most of these ingredients were smuggled from the prison kitchen or brought by a helpful correctional officer.

1. Combine the flour, sugar, baking powder, and salt in a large bowl. Mix well.
2. Stir in the egg, butter, and milk until the batter pours easily and is no longer lumpy. Add a little more milk if necessary. Mix in the Hershey kisses.
3. Heat the cooker and coat with a little vegetable oil.
4. Pour a small amount of batter onto the cooker. If cooking more than one, leave space between them.
5. Cook until bubbles form on top of the pancakes and they're dry around the edges. Slide a spatula underneath and flip.
6. Cook the other side for about the same amount of time. Serve immediately.

ALL BLOOD RUNS RED

In prison, races stick together. You'll see a bond here that doesn't quite exist in the same way out in the free world. The whites got a thing they call The Klan, the blacks got the muscle, and the Mexicans got the knives. However, when correctional officers mistreat or disrespect inmates, those inmates can unite in war against the officers. I'm talking inmates banding together, putting race issues aside.

There was one officer in particular who'd always abuse his power. He treated all inmates, all races, the same way—like shit. One day, he messed with the wrong convict. As he was escorting one particular homie out of the cellblock, this escorting officer punched the handcuffed convict right in the face. In seconds, all the nearby inmates who saw it happen—black, white, and Hispanic—jumped on the correctional officer. We were all tear-gassed and all the COs raced to the yard in an attempt to control what was turning into a full-on riot. The convict who had been punched while cuffed had Down syndrome, and he'd been like a little brother to everyone, made mistakes like everyone else. That day, in Corcoran, we all came together.

Standing alone and apart, we're nothing but puppets, but together we could do some good—even in prison. This Ramen & Bean Jambalaya seems like that. A mixture of odd ingredients apart, but when they come together, you get an amazing dish that blends beautifully.

RAMEN & BEAN JAMBALAYA

INGREDIENTS

2 packs any flavor Ramen

1½ cups boiling water

1 can (15 to 16 ounces) hot chili with beans

1 can (15 to 16 ounces) black beans, drained

1 summer sausage (about 9 ounces), chopped, or 1 can (9 ounces) Vienna sausage, drained and chopped

2 jalapeño chiles, chopped

Louisiana or other hot sauce

1. Crush the Ramen in the wrappers and empty into a bowl. Save the seasoning packets for another use.
2. Add the water, cover, and let it sit for 8 minutes.
3. Drain off excess water.
4. Mix the chili, black beans, sausage, and jalapeños in a microwavable bowl.
5. Add hot sauce to taste for an extra kick.
6. Cover and microwave for 3 to 5 minutes, until hot.
7. Add the Ramen. Mix well.

IN THE CIRCLE

There were many snowy nights in Tehachapi State Prison, when the homies and I would hang out around the handball court bleachers, sharing war stories from our youth and reminiscing about the hearts we broke along the way. Some of us were fathers, brothers, sons, and husbands. Some were short-timers, but most of the group were lifers. I was honored that these men would allow me to join their circle. Lifers don't usually socialize with short-timers. They stay away from guys who have parole dates. It's about disconnecting with the free world. Not having to hear "When I get out I'm going to . . ." or "I have just a few months left." These words don't fit in a lifer's vocabulary. There are some guys who mix well, of course, but it's totally up to the lifer who he allows in his circle.

The knowledge and wisdom I gained in prison can be credited to these men. From Big Topo, I learned to attack before I ever had to defend. His advice kept me alive in many questionable circumstances. Fred M. pointed out the key is to never stop learning. Seek out all the schooling you can—formal and informal. And from every lifer, I learned to appreciate my freedom. So, to this day, I find myself drinking a Cadillac every morning and thinking of the times I shared with them, surviving the hellhole, and trying to make sure I never go back.

CADILLAC COFFEE

INGREDIENTS

1 tablespoon instant coffee granules (preferably Taster's Choice or Folgers)

2 cups boiling water

2 tablespoons sugar

5 tablespoons French vanilla flavor creamer

3 tablespoons honey

1. Place the coffee in a very large mug.
2. Add the water and stir.
3. Add the sugar and creamer and stir.
4. Add the honey and stir some more.

Repeating the Lesson

Nine years after being released from prison, I ended up back on the same road to hell. I wasn't that naive eighteen-year-old from before. I was just shy of my thirty-third birthday. My tattoos, reminders of my past, had started to fade. I was an adult, a husband, and a father of three kids. I love my kids more than my life and did what any father would do to protect them. For me, that meant carrying a weapon to ward off attacks that often came by complete surprise. And that's what put me on another long vacation from society—and took me away from my kids.

When I found myself back in that cell, I knew what was coming next. Every moment, every day, my ability to keep cool would be tested. There would be riots, stabbings, and lockdowns. And when there was a lockdown, there would be no communication with my kids.

The shit that hurt the most? Getting letters from my kids. After the correctional officer would drop off the letters, it would take me a moment to open them up. The pain was too much just to see their handwriting. "Miss you Daddy. Please come home. I love you." The regret was a heavy load to carry. I kept from screaming by remembering the words of another man who had been incarcerated, Nelson Mandela: "There is no easy walk to freedom, anywhere, and many of us will have to pass through the valley of the shadow of death again and again before we reach the mountaintop of our desires."

P B & PLÁTANO SANDWICH SPREAD

INGREDIENTS

6 tablespoons peanut butter
6 slices bread
3 bananas, sliced
2 handfuls M&M's candy
3 tablespoons honey

1. Spread the peanut butter on each piece of bread.
2. Place the banana slices on top of each piece.
3. Sprinkle the M&M's over the banana slices.
4. Pour the honey over each slice of bread. Press the slices together to make 3 sandwiches.
5. Cut into quarters and serve.

NOT-SO-HAPPY HOLIDAYS

There's a lot of tension in prison around the end of the year. The weather gets colder, we start going outside less, and then the holidays arrive. They represent more of what we don't have. All it takes is for one idiot to lose it and start a wildfire. The spark that ignites it could be a bad call on the basketball court, or just a hard look. Anger, resentment, and sadness are released in the form of physical violence. But there were volunteers, particularly around the holidays, who'd bring a little joy, even to the coldest men. They would hold church services and then share some goodies and snacks—kind of like a Christmas party. They would also arrange for some of us to pick out toys and gifts that they would deliver to our families. It bordered on a feeling of normality, to know your kids would get a gift from Dad on Christmas. I will never forget the sound of my kids on the phone saying, "Thank you, Daddy!" on Christmas morning.

PEANUT BRITTLE

INGREDIENTS

1 tablespoon butter, plus more butter or vegetable oil for the pan

1 cup salted peanuts

1 cup sugar

½ cup corn syrup

½ teaspoon salt

1 teaspoon baking soda

1. Butter or oil an 8-by-8-inch square metal baking pan. Set aside.
2. Mix the peanuts, sugar, corn syrup, and salt in a large microwavable bowl.
3. Microwave for 7 to 8 minutes, stirring once or twice. It will bubble and get very hot.
4. Add the butter and microwave for 2 to 3 minutes more, until the mixture turns a caramel color.
5. Working quickly to avoid letting the brittle set, carefully remove the bowl from the microwave. Add the baking soda and stir until mixed well. It will bubble up even more and be very, very hot.
6. Carefully pour the mixture into the buttered pan. Jiggle the pan so the mixture spreads out evenly.
7. If you have the option, refrigerate the brittle so it cools faster. Otherwise, just let it sit for about 30 minutes until cool.
8. Break into pieces and serve.

GET FADED

Making prison hooch is a team effort. It takes seven long days to ferment the mix of smuggled ingredients. In a dorm facility, the only hiding place is a stall in the restroom. The last time I made it, my homies and I used my cell. As it brewed, I left the cell as little as possible.

On the sixth day, the smell was pretty strong and reaching beyond my cell walls. When the CO walked by, delivering mail, I thought my brewing days were over, but he kept on walking. Then he stopped, turned around, and waved the mail from side to side in front of his face. "It better be gone before my shift is over." Right away, I began to strain the pruno and pour it into all the empty tumblers I had. It was a day too early, but it would have to do.

Once the yard was open, I motioned to my other two homies that we had to start the party early! We wrapped bandanas around our tumblers and found an empty area around the baseball bleachers. Other homies started to show up; one brought a radio playing some old-school jams and another brought some smokes. Man, for a little while I didn't see the concrete wall that surrounded us or the gun tower just above us. Just hanging out with the homies, enjoying laughs and pouring out a bit of pruno to the ones we'd lost.

That night in my cell, I stunk like duck butter and pickle juice! Feeding the sharks and puking at the same time, it's hard to say it was worth it. Jailhouse hooch makes for a wicked hangover.

INGREDIENTS

20 oranges, cut in half

1 cup fruit punch drink

70 packets (1 teaspoon each) sugar (about 1½ cups total)

4 packets (0.39 ounces each) ketchup (about 3 tablespoons)

1 large slice bread (any kind—it provides the fermentation)

4 cups boiling water

1. Squeeze the oranges into a large, heavy-duty plastic bag, allowing a few orange pieces to fall into the bag. Do not use a zip-top or resealable bag; it will explode.

2. Add the fruit punch, sugar, ketchup, and bread.

3. Close the bag and tie a knot.

4. Remove the ink stick from a Bic pen. Use the empty chamber to poke a hole in the bag, leaving it in place. This will allow the pruno to breathe; otherwise, the bag might inflate and explode. A straw also works.

5. Place the bag in a bucket and pour the water around it. Cover the top of the bucket with a folded blanket or towel.

6. Once a day for the next 7 days, replace the hot water in the bucket. Keep it covered.

7. After a week, strain the pruno through a clean (or dirty) sock, removing the fruit clumps and bread. If you have a fine mesh strainer or cheesecloth, you're probably not in prison.

Hangover Cure

The Fish Bowl was a must after a long night of getting wasted, especially after drinking pruno. Usually, we didn't make pruno just for the hell of it. It was mostly for times of celebration—like a birthday or when a good friend is getting ready to parole. Sometimes these parties can end up really bad. When a lifer friend of mine we called Trouble was granted a release date, man, it was a party. Not only did we have pruno, but also a kitchen worker brought us a fifth of vodka. When you have a party with a bunch of opposing gang members, including killers, and serve pruno with vodka shots—it's all bad! These guys are sworn enemies on the street. A lot of blood has been shed between them, and once liquor gets involved, old grudges seem to surface.

Most of these parties are in the kitchen area, behind closed doors. Free staff and COs turn a blind eye to the very vicious fights between old enemies. When we beat one another up, the COs don't have to. Luckily, my friend Trouble didn't get too wasted. It would have been a shame if he'd lost his chance at freedom over some drunk night in prison.

After a night like this, I'd wake up with the nastiest hangover. That's when Plato de Pescado was a must. The spices in this dish clean you up and get you back on your toes.

PLATO DE PESCADO (FISH BOWL)

INGREDIENTS

1 pack shrimp flavor Ramen
¼ cup instant white rice
About 1½ cups boiling water
2 cans (4 ounces each) mackerel, drained
1 can (4 ounces) smoked oysters
1 summer sausage (about 9 ounces), chopped, or 1 can (9 ounces) Vienna sausage, drained and chopped
1 onion, chopped
2 jalapeño chiles, chopped
Pinch of garlic powder
4 tablespoons (¼ cup) strawberry jelly
6 tablespoons soy sauce
1 small bag (about 3 ounces) spicy pork skins or rinds

1. Crush the Ramen in the wrapper and empty into a microwavable bowl. Set aside the seasoning packet.
2. Add the rice. Add water until the rice and Ramen are submerged.
3. Cover, but leave a slight opening. Microwave for 10 to 12 minutes, until the rice and Ramen are soft.
4. Drain off excess water. Cover to keep warm.
5. Mix the mackerel, oysters, sausage, onion, jalapeños, seasoning, garlic powder, jelly, and soy sauce in a separate microwavable bowl.
6. Cover and microwave for about 6 minutes, until hot.
7. Add the pork skins and stir. Re-cover and microwave for 6 minutes more.
8. Serve on top of the Ramen-rice mixture.

Fire and Spirit

After years of doing time, and with plenty more to go, I was worn out and looking for a different way to get through the remainder. The will to get up every day was waning. Many of the homies around me dealt with their stress by abusing drugs. I couldn't go out like that—it just wasn't me. I confided in another inmate, Pastor Phil. I would pour out my troubles and worries, and he'd always have the right things to say.

He had a vision of preaching in every dorm of the Chino prison facility. This was something unheard of because of the prison gang politics, and doing this would put him at risk with the black and white inmates. He asked me to accompany him to preach and be an advocate to the other men who might be going through the same suffering I was. Even though I knew I'd get mean mug looks from the homies, I agreed to back Pastor Phil. He then asked for approval from the shotcallers to preach in the other dorms, and to our mutual surprise, he got it. It was settled.

The day before we were set to go into the first dorm, one of the biggest race riots in Chino occurred. Members of the most vicious gang were breaking down our doors, and we were trapped and outnumbered. Just about every other dorm had gone up in flames. Near the point of the door breaking in, the gang members were corralled by their seniors and told not to hurt us. It was unbelievable. We ended up making food and sharing a meal with some of the younger gang members.

Pastor Phil didn't get to preach the way he intended to, but a miracle occurred just the same.

PASTOR PHIL'S SWEET BURRITOS

INGREDIENTS

1 bag (8 ounces) instant white rice

2 cups hot water

3 summer sausages (about 9 ounces each), chopped, or 3 cans (9 ounces each) Vienna sausage, drained and chopped

3 pouches or cans (11 ounces each) cooked roast beef, chopped

1 can (16 ounces) refried beans

20 packets (1 teaspoon each) sugar (a little less than ½ cup total)

4 tablespoons (¼ cup) soy sauce

6 to 8 large flour tortillas

Sriracha sauce and/or mayonnaise

1. Combine the rice and water in a large microwavable bowl and stir.
2. Cover and microwave for 5 minutes or as directed on the package.
3. Mix the sausages, roast beef, refried beans, sugar, and soy sauce in a separate microwavable bowl.
4. Cover and microwave for 8 to 10 minutes, until hot.
5. Warm the tortillas in the microwave for 30 seconds.
6. Divide the rice evenly among the tortillas. Divide the filling over the rice and roll into burritos.

NOTE:

- Before you wrap up the burritos, try adding a shot of sriracha sauce and/or mayonnaise.
- These burritos pair well with small yellow chiles, nacho chips, and cold cola.

WASTED DAYS, WASTED NIGHTS

My birthdays in my twenties and most of my thirties were spent in prison. For my twenty-first birthday, I was working in the mess hall as a line server. Because I was the youngest of the crew, they treated me like a little brother, and of course, as their little brother, I had to endure plenty of practical jokes. Once, I left the line to go feed the sharks, and they snuck into the restroom with a trash can full of ice water! I didn't even need to wipe my ass, they soaked me so completely. I thought that was my birthday present! But after a good laugh, they surprised me with this cake. It wasn't the twenty-first birthday I'd imagined I'd have when I was a little kid, but it's one I will always remember. Most of the men were lifers and probably will never get to celebrate any birthdays with their sons or brothers. My birthday cheered them up quite a bit, and that was okay with me.

DING DONG CAKE

INGREDIENTS

12 chocolate cupcakes, wrappers removed
1 jar (18 ounces) Goober peanut butter–jelly mix
1 bag (6 ounces) mixed nuts

NOTE: Nothing beats washing this down with some cold milk.

1. Place 8 of the cupcakes on a plate in a tight circle so that they're all touching.
2. Place the remaining 4 cupcakes in the center, on top, so that it has the shape of a cake.
3. Spread the peanut butter and jelly mix all over the cake as icing. Microwaving the open jar softens it up and makes it more spreadable.
4. Crush the nuts in the bag. Sprinkle over the cake.

Sweetening the Hard Times

The first time I saw this candy was at the Tehachapi Prison. There was this guy, Jimbo, an older white dude who would sell just about anything and everything. He was always telling us that he could sell water to a fish. One time I noticed him walking around the prison yard with small baggies filled with this hard-time candy. He would sell them for two packs of Ramen per bag of candy. At first I was hesitant to try it, but like all good salesmen, he gave me a taste for free, and well, I was hooked! In prison, we all become hustlers, doing what we can to get by.

HARD-TIME CANDY

INGREDIENTS

3 tablespoons presweetened cherry Kool-Aid powder
2 drops sriracha or other hot sauce

1. Put the Kool-Aid powder in a small bowl. Add the hot sauce.

2. Mix the Kool-Aid powder and hot sauce with a spoon, working the liquid into every granule of the powder. When it's combined, flip it like a pancake and continue to press it with the spoon to spread the hot sauce evenly.

3. Repeat flipping and pressing until it forms a hard, nickel-size lump. Try not to add more liquid until you've worked it for a while and it solidifies.

1. For additional pieces of candy, repeat with more Kool-Aid and hot sauce.

Pardon by the Governor

During my time in prison, I had the pleasure of seeing two lifers get released. The first one I met was just over fifty-five years old and had served thirty years in prison. I rarely talked to him on the yard because he mostly kept to himself. But the other was a good friend of mine who I got to know while I was at Corcoran. We called him Old Man Tony, and he served twenty-eight years before he was pardoned by the governor. He was a great storyteller and was often surrounded on the bleachers of the handball court, talking to homies about old times. He always had a good sense of humor and would say things like, "This is my house, and you kids are just visiting" or complain about the young kids by saying, "Stinking Pepsi generation." When he got the news of his pardon, he didn't look happy or even surprised. He told us he'd believe it when it happened. Well, a few months later that day happened. Two men were pardoned and released from many decades of prison. The day he left, the whole yard—blacks, whites, Hispanics, and even the COs—gave him a standing ovation as he walked across the yard toward the parole gate. The look on Old Man Tony's face was of a person about to face the greatest challenge in his life. It's very rare to see a lifer go home. One guy said, "It's like Halley's Comet, once in a great while."

PAROLE DAY CHEESECAKE

INGREDIENTS

1 bag (12 ounces) crunchy chocolate chip cookies
6 packets (1 ounce each) cream cheese (¾ cup total)
2 tablespoons honey
2 tablespoons French vanilla flavor creamer
1 packet Sweet'N Low
¾ cup presweetened Kool-Aid powder
(any flavor—a red flavor looks better than green or yellow)

1. Crumble the cookies into small pieces. You should have about 3 cups.
2. Pour the crumbs into a shallow microwavable bowl. Spread them around with a spoon to create a cookie crust.
3. Microwave for 3 to 4 minutes, until the crust is golden brown. Set aside to cool.
4. Mix the cream cheese, honey, creamer, Sweet'N Low, and Kool-Aid in a separate bowl until smooth.
5. Pour the cheese mixture over the crust.
6. Cover the cheesecake and place in the refrigerator or an ice-filled bucket for 4 to 5 hours, until solid.

Author Bios

GUSTAVO "GOOSE" ALVAREZ was born in Guadalajara, Jalisco, Mexico. Raised in West Los Angeles, he was in and out of juvenile and adult correctional facilities for various crimes from ages sixteen to thirty-nine. While serving time in Tehachapi State Prison, he became a part of a mentorship program for at-risk kids called S.E.E.K., and successfully completed a twelve-step recovery program. In May 2013, he was released from federal prison and has never looked back.

CLIFTON COLLINS JR. is a native Angeleno and has been acting since 1987, when he appeared in his first movie, *One Eight Seven*, opposite Samuel L. Jackson. He has played everything from a gay Mexican hit man in the movie *Traffic* to a Vietnam-era Southern soldier in *Tigerland* to the character Romeo in the film *The Boondock Saints II: All Saints Day*. He is particularly well known for his portrayal of Perry Smith, the killer who was the object of writer Truman Capote's obsession in *Capote*. He also voiced the fictional video game character Cesar Vialpando in *Grand Theft Auto: San Andreas*.